Daniel Henderson has touched on a subject that is of the highest importance to the church and immeasurably valued by our God. There is simply too much ignorance and misunderstanding surrounding the person and power of the Holy Spirit. I thank God for this book; it serves as a teacher to those who are ignorant, but also empowerment to those who are floundering. I strongly recommend *Transforming Presence*, written by a man who lives what he has written and has exercised Spirit-given influence upon the church.

ROBBIE SYMONS
Pastor, Harvest Bible Chapel, Oakville, Ontario; Bible teacher for 100 Huntley Street; author of *Passion Cry*

Transforming Presence threads the needle of biblical truth, vibrant Christianity, and a hunger for renewal. Drawing on years of ministry across a broad array of denominations and traditions, Daniel Henderson challenges readers to consider—or reconsider—how the Holy Spirit works from the inside-out. This book is a wonderful blend of depth and balance. It presents a common ground vision for what every Christian and every church desperately needs.

MARK VROEGOP
Lead Pastor, College Park Church, Indianapolis

Is there a more pressing issue for believers than understanding how the Holy Spirit moves and works in our lives? I can't think of one. And yet the church landscape today is filled with enough poor theology and bad lingo to confuse just about any believer. Daniel Henderson is the codebreaker. With great ease and simplicity, Daniel sets our sights on the ministry of the Holy Spirit through the ultimate lens of the new covenant and equips us to pray to, worship, and think about the Spirit with much more clarity and relevance. To call this book revolutionary for growing disciples probably wouldn't be an overstatement. Thank you Daniel.

WILL DAVIS JR.
Founding and Senior Pastor, Austin Christian Fellowship
Author of *Enough: Finding More by Living with Less*

Buckle in. This book is going to challenge some of your assumptions, ideas, and practices you have regarding the Holy Spirit. Words create worlds. That old axiom is especially relevant to this book. The words we sing, preach, and pray about the Holy Spirit shape our understanding of who He is and what He does. This biblical and compelling work by Daniel Henderson will help you align your beliefs and your practices. And it will give you a fresh appreciation for the incredible gift of the Holy Spirit that has taken up permanent residence in you.

LANCE WITT
Pastor and Leadership Coach
Author of *Replenish: Leading from a Healthy Soul*

Every worship pastor/leader needs to read this book. As a worship pastor, it was so refreshing to finally read a book that does not tiptoe around certain "ambiguities" regarding the Holy Spirit, but rather speaks directly into them. You can't sing intentions. As a result, our words greatly matter in worship because people remember words. Daniel Henderson does a great job of capturing biblical truth of the Holy Spirit from a New Testament lens. This will strengthen your understanding of the Holy Spirit, and your desire to honor Him with the language used.

JUSTIN SCHWARZENTRAUB
Worship Pastor, Brave Church, Denver, CO

Perhaps nothing would profit our own souls and our local church ministries more than knowing and applying carefully the Bible's teaching about the new covenant and the Holy Spirit. Here is a book that will help us with this. It presents what the Bible teaches and what it doesn't, but it does this gently with a pastoral spirit. Reading it is soul-refreshing. The chapter on the relationship of the Holy Spirit to music, and the appendix on a new covenant worship vocabulary, are in themselves reasons enough to buy this book and devour it. Highly recommended.

LARRY PETTEGREW
Systematic Theology Professor, The Shepherd's Seminary
Author, *The New Covenant Ministry of the Holy Spirit*

In Daniel's new book, *Transforming Presence*, he states, "Let's keep the plumb line of God's purpose in mind. The Holy Spirit was given to glorify Jesus in our hearts, minds, and actions; in our homes and relationships; in our service, fellowship, and worship in His church." No matter your theological perspective on the role and ministry of the Holy Spirit, this volume will challenge you, encourage you and cause you to desire a fresh touch of renewal from the gracious hand of our Lord. Please read it with an open mind, heart, and spiritual eyes.

S. LINDSAY TAYLOR
President, Strategic Renewal Canada

I believe this book is the beginning of a much needed conversation and should inform and recalibrate worship leaders toward truth about the third person of the Trinity. Worship leaders are theologians, and when they lead, their commentary, exhortations, and prompts are training others how to view the Holy Spirit. Henderson removes the esotericism that's often associated with the third person of the Trinity and offers a clear, biblical foundation that should not only challenge how we think about the Holy Spirit but how we publicly speak about Him as well. This is required reading for anyone called to lead worship.

TRAVIS DOUCETTE
Pastor of Worship and Leadership Development, Harvest Bible Chapel Naples

Praise for *Transforming Presence*

Transforming Presence is the best book on the work of the Holy Spirit to appear in this century. It is biblically accurate, theologically solid, and perfectly balanced. Daniel Henderson rightly understands the person and work of the Holy Spirit from a compelling new covenant perspective. He challenges believers to fully grasp the work of the Spirit within our hearts, our lives, and our ministries. Don't miss it—you will be blessed from the inside out!

ED HINDSON
Founding Dean | Distinguished Professor of Religion
Rawlings School of Divinity–Liberty University

It's so easy to settle in to assumptions that pass for theology. Glossy phrases, catchy lyrics, oft-repeated slogans work their way into our ideas of truth without the foundational work of studying and applying scriptural truth. Certainly our deep understanding of the work and person of the Holy Spirit has suffered from being the subject of such tropes. Daniel Henderson challenges us to address our assumptions and line them up with eternal truth revealed in the Word of God. With Scripture as the linchpin, this book leads us to a helpful reexamination, and every reader will be richer for it. Nothing can be more valuable for our lives than a deep and true understanding of the Holy Spirit.

JENNIFER KENNEDY DEAN
Author of *Live a Praying Life*
Executive Director of The Praying Life Foundation

It's true that Christianity is hopeless without the Holy Spirit. Daniel Henderson places that fact front and center in his new book, *Transforming Presence*. Most of us know that pardon from sin is only through Jesus Christ. What's desperately needed today is the faith that *all* power is in the Holy Spirit.

JIM CYMBALA
Senior Pastor, The Brooklyn Tabernacle
Author of *Fresh Wind, Fresh Fire*

Transforming Presence is provocative and compelling. For too long many in evangelical circles have had an uneasy alliance with the Holy Spirit. Daniel makes the bold cry for the church to be open to the work of the Spirit, for without Him we can do nothing. As Christian leaders we need to be sure to understand and speak of the work of the Holy Spirit with a clear new covenant perspective.

BECKY HARLING
Speaker, Leadership Coach, and author of *Who Do You Say That I Am?*

I trust Daniel Henderson to teach me about the Holy Spirit because I have repeatedly experienced God's Spirit through Daniel's ministry and because Daniel always takes everything back to Scripture. What a great book on the Holy Spirit in the new covenant!

JIM LEGGETT
Senior Pastor, Grace Fellowship, Katy, TX

Daniel's exhortation to be led and strengthened by the Holy Spirit is a timely word for every minister and leader. This book is a culmination of his experience and a natural outflow of his ministry. *Transforming Presence* will be an encouragement to leaders everywhere, refocusing us on the power source of our lives.

AL TOLEDO
Lead Pastor, Chicago Tabernacle

This book will change the way many—from both cessationist and continuationist perspectives—think about the person and work of the Holy Spirit. But even if you find yourself already in agreement with the theological foundations of *Transforming Presence*, it will almost certainly change the way you speak of the ministry of the Spirit. This is valuable teaching for every Christian, but I especially recommend it to pastors and worship leaders.

DONALD S. WHITNEY
Professor of Biblical Spirituality and Associate Dean at The Southern Baptist Theological Seminary, Louisville, KY; author of *Spiritual Disciplines for the Christian Life* and *Praying the Bible*.

Daniel's book on prayer, *Old Paths, New Power*, was the most convicting and encouraging book I have read on this topic—and one I continue to recommend to Christian leaders at every opportunity. His teaching on the person and the work of the Holy Spirit is equally beneficial and just as needed for the church today.

STEVEN KRYGER
CommunicateJesus.com

Old truth seen with new eyes. *Transforming Presence* cuts through familiar traditions, personal biases, and cultural slants to open our eyes anew to the wildly life-changing reality of the indwelling Holy Spirit. Thoroughly biblical. Personally transformational. Refreshingly life-giving.

TIM HAWKS
Lead Pastor, Hill Country Bible Church, Austin, Texas
Christ Together Directional Team Member

It's about time someone was courageous enough to reintroduce the Holy Spirit to the church as if He were a real person. Not some theological abstraction, emotional genie, or, worse yet, a strange gaseous vapor. And it's way past time for someone to step up and challenge the church—and those of us who lead her—to stop insulting the Spirit by the way we pray, rattle off clichés, mindlessly sing, and, in general, speak in reference to God the Spirit. If we ever truly hope to involve the Holy Spirit in our lives and ministries, this book by Daniel Henderson is, hands down, required reading.

STEPHEN DAVEY
Pastor/Teacher, Colonial Baptist Church
President, Shepherds Theological Seminary

TRANSFORMING
PRESENCE

TRANSFORMING PRESENCE

*How the Holy Spirit
Changes Everything —
From the Inside Out*

DANIEL HENDERSON

MOODY PUBLISHERS

CHICAGO

Unless otherwise indicated, Scripture quotations are from The Holy Bible, English Standard Version® (ESV®), copyright © 2001, 2007 by Crossway, a publishing ministry of Good News Publishers. Used by permission. All rights reserved.

Scripture quotations marked NKJV are taken from the New King James Version. Copyright © 1982 by Thomas Nelson. Used by permission. All rights reserved.

Scripture quotations marked CEB are taken from the Common English Bible® Copyright © 2010, 2011 by Common English Bible.™ Used by permission. All rights reserved worldwide. The "CEB" and "Common English Bible" trademarks are registered in the United States Patent and Trademark Office by Common English Bible. Use of either trademark requires the permission of Common English Bible.

Scripture quotations marked KJV are taken from the King James Version.

Scripture quotations marked MSG are from The Message, copyright © by Eugene H. Peterson 1993, 1994, 1995, 1996, 2000, 2001, 2002. Used by permission of Tyndale House Publishers, Inc.

Scripture quotations marked NLT are taken from the Holy Bible, New Living Translation, copyright © 1996, 2004, 2007 by Tyndale House Foundation. Used by permission of Tyndale House Publishers, Inc., Carol Stream, Illinois 60188. All rights reserved.

Scripture quotations marked NASB are taken from the New American Standard Bible®, Copyright © 1960, 1962, 1963, 1968, 1971, 1972, 1973, 1975, 1977, 1995 by The Lockman Foundation. Used by permission. (www.Lockman.org)

All emphasis to Scripture has been added.

Edited by Connor Sterchi
Interior design: Ragont Design
Cover design: Erik M. Peterson
Cover photo of bird-shaped lights copyright © 2018 by Adam-F / Lightstock (55810). All rights reserved.
Author photo: Kelly Weaver Photography

Library of Congress Cataloging-in-Publication Data

Names: Henderson, Daniel (Pastor) author.
Title: Transforming presence : how the Holy Spirit changes everything--from the inside out / Daniel Henderson.
Description: Chicago : Moody Publishers, 2018. | Includes bibliographical references.
Identifiers: LCCN 2018009909 (print) | LCCN 2018020030 (ebook) | ISBN 9780802496553 (ebook) | ISBN 9780802416957
Subjects: LCSH: Holy Spirit.
Classification: LCC BT121.3 (ebook) | LCC BT121.3 .H45 2018 (print) | DDC 231/.3--dc23
LC record available at https://lccn.loc.gov/2018009909

We hope you enjoy this book from Moody Publishers. Our goal is to provide high-quality, thought-provoking books and products that connect truth to your real needs and challenges. For more information on other books and products that will help you with all your important relationships, go to www.moodypublishers.com or write to:

Moody Publishers
820 N. LaSalle Boulevard
Chicago, IL 60610

3 5 7 9 10 8 6 4 2

Printed in the United States of America

This book is dedicated to the Regional Resource Leaders of The 6:4 Fellowship. These pastors are the devoted ground troops for a significant and Christ-honoring expansion of Scripture-fed, Spirit-led, worship-based prayer in churches across North America, and the world. While we all pray for the "fruits" of revival, these servant-leaders are catalysts for developing the "roots" of revival as they challenge their ministry colleagues to become praying pastors who lead praying churches. (Learn more at http://www.64fellowship.com)

CONTENTS

Foreword   15

Introduction: What We All Want   19

TEN VITAL PRACTICES FOR
A NEW EXPERIENCE OF THE HOLY SPIRIT

PRACTICE 1: Agree to Evaluate Your Assumptions   31

PRACTICE 2: Embrace the Holy Spirit's Primary Purpose   43

PRACTICE 3: Live in the Power of the New Covenant   57

PRACTICE 4: Pursue the Indwelling Person, Not an
External "Presence"   75

PRACTICE 5: Worship Like *You* Are the "House of the Lord"   93

PRACTICE 6: Experience the God Who Already "Showed Up"   111

PRACTICE 7: Seek a "Filling," Not a "Falling"   131

PRACTICE 8: Filter the Message in the Music   147

PRACTICE 9: Enjoy the Gift of Biblical Emotion   163

PRACTICE 10: Maximize Your New Covenant Life Plan   181

Conclusion: Pursuing the Hope of a New Covenant Revival   199

Appendix 1: Accurately Applying the Actions of Acts   209

Appendix 2: A New Covenant Worship Vocabulary   215

Notes   219

Acknowledgments   233

CHECK OUT

www.transformingpresencebook.com

WHERE YOU WILL FIND:

Video introductions and small group
discussion guides, and recorded prayers
by Daniel Henderson for each chapter

SPECIAL ARTICLES ON TOPICS LIKE:

The Balance of the Spirit and the Word

The Work of the Holy Spirit in the
Old Testament

Facts About the Deity of the Holy Spirit

AND MUCH MORE . . .

FOREWORD

The filling of the Spirit is, in some circles, a controversial, divisive, and misunderstood ministry of the Holy Spirit. Ask any Christian what it means to be filled with the Spirit. The answer may reflect ignorance, fear, speculation, fanaticism, or indifference. Why is there so much confusion about Spirit-infilling? Two reasons: *no teaching* and *wrong teaching*.

That's why I am excited about Daniel Henderson's insightful contribution in *Transforming Presence*. He does not argue doctrinal theories. The point of his book is simple, practical, and life-changing: you must understand the great truth of the indwelling of the Holy Spirit, then be filled with the Spirit to be a devoted, growing, and fruitful Christian.

We all know that it is a tragedy to live and die and go to hell without Christ. But we must affirm that it is also a tragedy to live and die and go to heaven without being filled with the Spirit. It is like getting a new car without figuring out how to start it. You might just put it in neutral and push it around everywhere you go. It does not have to be that way. You can be what God wants you to be, do what God wants you to do, and have what God wants you to have. But you must be filled with the Spirit. The human spirit fails unless the Holy Spirit fills.

I am reminded of the story of a group of pastors who had planned a citywide evangelistic campaign. The pastors favorably discussed the possibility of inviting the famous preacher, D. L. Moody, to be the speaker. But one young pastor complained, "From the way some of you talk, you would think Mr. Moody had a monopoly on the Holy Spirit." "No," another pastor replied, "Mr. Moody does not have a monopoly on the Spirit. But the Holy Spirit has a monopoly on Mr. Moody!"

Daniel Henderson has written this book to help you get to the place where the indwelling Holy Spirit has a monopoly on you, your family, and your church. Daniel's approach is distinctively gospel oriented and will give you practical insights on how to live in the power and practicality of the new covenant because of all Jesus has done for you.

It's been said that "If you have the Spirit without the Word, you will blow up. If you have the Word without the Spirit, you will dry up. If you have the Word and the Spirit, you will grow up." Daniel wants to help you find that balance as you grow up in the fullness of Jesus Christ, by the power of the Holy Spirit.

It is my joy to recommend this book to you as you discover a truly new, yet very biblical, experience of the Holy Spirit.

PASTOR H.B. CHARLES

"Nevertheless, I tell you the truth: it is to your advantage that I go away, for if I do not go away, the Helper will not come to you. But if I go, I will send him to you." —Jesus (John 16:7)

"If we review the history of the Church, we notice how many important truths, clearly revealed in Scripture, have been allowed to lie dormant for centuries, unknown and unappreciated except by a few isolated Christians, until it pleased God to enlighten the Church by chosen witnesses, and to bestow on His children the knowledge of hidden and forgotten treasures. . . . For how long a period, even after the Reformation, was the doctrine of the Holy Ghost and His work in conversion, and His indwelling in the believer, almost unknown!"
—Adolph Saphir, A Jewish Presbyterian Missionary (1831–1891)

"When believers live in the power of the Spirit, the evidence in their lives is supernatural. The church cannot help but be different, and the world cannot help but notice."
—Francis Chan

"In our preaching and in our practice [the Holy Spirit] does not hold that place of prominence that He has in God's plan and in His promises. While our creed on the Holy Spirit is orthodox and scriptural, His presence and power in the life of believers, in the ministry of the Word, in the witness of the Church to the world, is not what the Word promises or God's plan requires."
—Andrew Murray

Introduction

WHAT WE ALL WANT

O ver a hundred church members paid good money, took time off work, and made a leap of faith to follow their pastor into the unknown. Would they discover new heights of spiritual exhilaration or more depths of disappointment with an oversold renewal event? The gathering promised to be an "out-of-the-box" experience. No one really knew what we were getting into. The leader was not even sure. I know because I was their pastor.

The experience of leading my first "prayer summit" was unforgettable. As I drove from Sacramento toward a rather Spartan camp in the Sierra-Nevada mountains, my mind raced with questions. Every heartbeat seemed to pulsate with fresh nuances of self-doubt.

We would gather from Wednesday evening to Saturday noon in an unscripted prayer experience, with absolutely no agenda. The only "scheduled" components were the meal times, to honor the camp hosts. We would establish some basic guidelines, then launch into thirty concentrated hours (apart from eating and sleep) of spontaneous Scripture reading, a capella singing, prayer, confession, fellowship—and fresh spiritual discovery.

A SPIRITUAL PINNACLE

The pinnacle of the three days was a multi-hour communion service on the final evening. A simple table positioned in the middle of the room hosted juice, bread, and a few candles. We sat in concentric circles around this centerpiece. The next two-and-a-half hours were filled with spontaneous readings by dozens of believers from the Scriptures about the person and work of Christ. We sang classic hymns blended with new songs about the cross. Feeling no time constraints, church members were able to worship deeply, confess sins, seek relational reconciliation. We would eventually hold, cherish, and partake of the communion elements with profound love and worship for Jesus.

The evening culminated as we gathered shoulder-to-shoulder around the table. Radiant faces, many lined with tears of joy, looked upward in these final moments of indescribable worship. In the concluding moments we sang all four verses of the treasured hymn "All Hail the Power of Jesus Name." It felt like an intense sampler of heaven. Pure hearts and unified souls experienced the gospel like never before. The Holy Spirit was palpable in our midst. All of us were truly transformed.

UNPRECEDENTED IMPACT

As we wrapped up on Saturday afternoon, these exceptional days had proven to be the closest thing to a real taste of spiritual revival that any of us had ever experienced. The combination of multiple large group sessions, small group prayer times, and quiet personal moments were woven together into a tapestry of unprecedented intimacy with Jesus. In these hours, new believers and longtime

Christians worshiped like never before. Individuals had been delivered from lifelong habitual sin, marriages were restored, beautiful racial reconciliation occurred, people felt called to full-time ministry, and a new level of organic unity was profoundly evident. We experienced an unprecedented, transforming work of the indwelling Spirit.

It seemed that the goals a pastor typically scripts for his five-year ministry plan all converged in just three days. We did not post any Facebook Live reports. (Actually, Facebook did not yet exist.) We simply cherished this holy experience, discovered in the remote woods of Northern California. We came to understand that when we give the Lord our undivided attention, He is more than glad to oblige.

Since that first summit, I've led almost a hundred similar experiences across the nation. We've gathered at retreat centers, church buildings, and even hotels, with various groups of 15 to 225. The dynamics differ each time because of the unique combination the participants, various environments, the distinctive mix of Scripture readings, and the fresh blend of spontaneous singing. Yet the reality is always the same. The Holy Spirit works palpably and powerfully in accomplishing His gospel purposes in us and among us. We taste real transformation. We leave more like Jesus and become more passionately reengaged in His mission in this world.

BACK TO REALITY

In these environments, we consistently experience the untainted sufficiency of the Word of God, the Spirit of God, and the people of God. This happens without elevated platforms, featured personalities, slick productions, printed run sheets, or prede-termined programming cues. No computerized lights or smoke machines stimulate our senses. We cherish a level of community beyond our typical Sunday experience. Dozens, even hundreds of Scripture passages fill our minds. The Holy Spirit takes dynamic control of our hearts and our agenda. Christ is profoundly exalted.

Most often, as the summits conclude, participants wonder how the time passed so quickly. They leave with an extraordinary spiritual hunger for an even greater work of the Holy Spirit in their lives. I remember one longtime member announcing to the group, "Now we have to go back to reality." I quickly countered, "No. *This* is reality. Our mission is to integrate this experience in the day-to-day patterns of our lives." The transforming presence of the Holy Spirit can and must be the experience of every believer.

SEEKING BUT NOT FINDING?

For many years as a pastor and avid student of the Bible, the "lead-ing of the Spirit" had been a theological concept, tucked away in my neatly categorized seminary file. Over these years, through the prayer summits and many other experiences, the leadership of the Holy Spirit has become a treasured interchange with an intimate friend, a divine tutor, living and ruling in my heart. The Spirit's purposes are becoming more clear to me—to take the Word of Christ and make it real to the people of Christ so they would honor the person of Christ in the mission of Christ for the glory of Christ.

This is what every true Christian longs to experience—not just in an extended time away from the busyness of life, but through weekly worship services and in the regular and the mun-dane rhythms of daily living. We all long for and desperately need transformation. In various seasons of life, we battle spiritual apathy, destructive attitudes, ungodly habits, strained relationships and the burdensome emotions of doubt, fear, and discouragement. Lasting inside-out change can happen because of what Jesus promised us in the person and power of His Holy Spirit.

> **This is what every true Christian longs to experience—not just in an extended time away from the busyness of life, but through weekly worship services and in the regular and the mundane rhythms of daily living.**

The good news is that you do not need to go to a prayer summit to experience this promise. However, most Christians are starving for this reality but not finding it in the current paradigms we embrace in modern Christianity.

SPIRITUAL FAKE NEWS

"Fake news" has emerged as *the* news in recent days. Media wars are an everyday occurrence. The average consumer is caught in the crossfire and left bewildered about the interactions and events that did or did not happen. Fake news about fake news about fake news seems to inundate the American public. Frustrating indeed.

Today, could it be that we are being influenced by fake news about the person and work of the Holy Spirit? As you read that, maybe your instinct is put up your guard. But let's be honest and ask an important question: "Is everything we sing about and hear in church an accurate representation of what the Holy Spirit has said about Himself? Does it accurately portray His profound promises and plans for our lives as New Testament believers?" Like a third grader standing for the first time on the rim of the Grand Canyon, having only before seen pictures, we would do well to ponder anew the realities of the Holy Spirit—with eyes, mind, and heart wide open.

These recent years of biblical discovery, presented in this book, have brought profound growth in my spiritual life. My study has exposed some misguided views I previously believed and expressed about the work of the Spirit. It was never my intention to teach things that were unclear or inaccurate. I was just repeating ideas I'd heard in church over the years. It is not easy when our long-held and deeply cherished assumptions are confronted.

LOOKING THROUGH A GOSPEL LENS

I wear prescription bifocals, so I see the world through lenses. For decades, I have read and understood the Bible through a unique set of lenses as well. We all see the world and, yes, even Scripture, through lenses. Our lenses are composed of our traditions, our experiences, our denominational backgrounds, our loyalty to particular doctrinal camps, our culture, and our own partial understanding. We know we need to see the Bible and our Christian experience through the pure lens of clear biblical teaching—but it is not always easy. In today's information age, with unprecedented and often unfiltered messages permeating our beliefs, the need for clarity is greater than ever.

Let me admit up front that the litmus test I've used in this book is the gospel. This lens empowers us to enjoy the fullness of the finished work of Jesus Christ in the person of the Holy Spirit.

When Jesus sat with His disciples in the upper room, prior

to His death, burial, and resurrection, He announced, "This cup that is poured out for you is the new covenant in my blood" (Luke 22:20). In so doing He laid down a leading indicator that *everything* was about to change. The Bible makes it very clear that this new covenant made the old covenant fulfilled. It is superior in every way. We will unpack this in more detail later.

One profound and paramount change effected by the finished work of Christ is the way we experience and relate to God's Spirit. The gospel is the new and powerful lens through which we see and experience the transforming presence of the Spirit of God.

In the Old Testament, God's presence led His people in the form of a cloud by day and a fire by night. In the New Testament, the cloud and the fire are within us through the presence of the Holy Spirit. In the old covenant, the presence of God filled the tabernacle and later the temple in Jerusalem. In the new covenant, we are the temple. His Spirit fills us. Jesus did not die to sanctify and fill buildings or "atmospheres." His work on the cross changed everything. He died to cleanse, fill, and empower our human hearts. His work is inside-out, not the previous "outside-in" paradigm of the old covenant. This is the promise of ongoing transformation. We actually enjoy a *new* experience of the Holy Spirit because of the gospel. Our language and practice can and must reflect the reality of these amazing privileges.

INSIDE-OUT TRANSFORMATION

The apostle Paul was emphatic in explaining the transforming power of a new covenant experience of the indwelling Holy Spirit. He gave us this promise, "And we all, with unveiled face, beholding the glory of the Lord, are being transformed into the same image from one degree of glory to another. For this comes from the Lord who is the Spirit" (2 Cor. 3:18). A few verses later, he explained, "For God, who said, 'Let light shine out of darkness,' has shone *in our hearts* to give the light of the knowledge of the glory of God in the face of Jesus Christ" (2 Cor. 4:6). He explained, "for it is God who works *in* you, both to will and to work for his good pleasure" (Phil. 2:13). He assured us that God is "able to do far more abundantly than all that we ask or think, according to the power at work *within* us" (Eph. 3:20). He summarized the indwelling power of God by declaring, "Christ in you, the hope of glory" (Col. 1:27).

My growing understanding and experience of the work of the Holy Spirit from a new covenant perspective has been a game-changer, both delightful and disarming. I've found a new longing to be taught again. I've needed the humility to subject my experience to the Word of God rather than subjecting the Word of God to my experience and previous ideas. I hope this will be your discovery as well.

Today, my heart embraces an unprecedented freedom and clarity to walk in the power of the Holy Spirit, based on His very words about who He is and what He wants to do in my life for the glory of Jesus Christ. My weekend worship experiences continue to be transformed. A fresh set of lenses is giving me a new experience of the Holy Spirit.

I believe the need is urgent for every believer to experience the person and power of the Spirit from a clear inside-out, distinctly new covenant, perspective. We would never teach other primary doctrines in ways that diminish the primacy of the gospel. We are resolute—and rightly so—to teach about Christ, sin, salvation, church life, the end times, and other core doctrines through a new covenant lens. Yet when it comes to the Holy Spirit, it seems as if many believers and ministry leaders are still wearing Old Testament glasses and speaking in ways that diminish the implications of the cross and, thus, breed confusion in our experience of the Holy Spirit. But the good news can trump any and all of our fake news.

HOLY HEARTBURN

After decades as a senior pastor, I have spent the last ten years speaking to hundreds of thousands of believers in churches across North America. These congregations have represented a broad variety of theological persuasions. Like a low-grade heartburn, what I have heard and witnessed in my travels became quite unsettling. These consistent observations have stirred me to write *Transforming Presence* in hopes of clarifying some sincerely stated but potentially "fake news" about the Holy Spirit.

> **I have written this book not to question your experience of the Holy Spirit, but to challenge you to think of His work more clearly and speak from His Word more biblically so you can experience His transforming power *in* your life more consistently.**

I have written this book not to question your experience of the Holy Spirit, but to challenge you to think of His work more clearly and speak from His Word more biblically so you can experience His transforming power in your life more consistently. And as I write, I am hopeful. Christians across the spiritual landscape are earnest and eager to know and experience the Holy Spirit.

WHAT YOU WON'T FIND IN THIS BOOK

Let me clarify what this book is *not* about. We will not address some of the more divisive arguments that are common concerning the work of the Holy Spirit. You will not find any discussion about speaking in tongues, the baptism of the Holy Spirit, or opinions about healing and miracles. I have treasured friends and ministry colleagues on both sides of these debates. Writers much more astute than me have unpacked these matters with great insight. We will not spend significant energy going after fringe teachers by name, but we will identify some teachings that might be derailing an extraordinary authentic New Testament experience of the Holy Spirit.

This book is for anyone hungering for a deep, fresh, and profound work of the Spirit of God in their personal life and church experience. If nothing less than God's very best will satisfy the hunger of your soul, then I pray I can help lead you there.

OUR COMMON PURSUIT

We all want the same thing: a true, biblical, transforming, Christ-honoring experience of the indwelling Spirit of God. And our society desperately needs the *real* thing. Younger generations are turning away from the church faster than any other age group, with a third of Americans between 18 and 35 choosing no affiliation with religion.[1] Instead, many are being drawn to astrology and the occult.[2]

We cannot afford to keep "putting our best flesh forward" through a reliance on the mega-tools of modern ministry. Nor can we embrace any kind of quasi-mystical, extrabiblical misrepresentation of the power of the Holy Spirit. We must reawaken our understanding and resolve to experience the promise of "Christ in you, the hope of glory" (Col. 1:27) for the sake of a culture that is confused and held captive by darkness.

The good news is that our Lord Jesus Christ wants the best for us—more than we want it for ourselves. His Spirit can empower us again to "turn the world upside down" (see Acts 17:6) through the message of the gospel. I pray this book will equip us to align with His desires. Let us embrace the truth of all He has destined for us through a distinctly gospel experience of His indwelling, transforming presence.

Pastor Jim Cymbala writes, "The Holy Spirit is God's agent on earth, yet he is the least understood . . . member of the Trinity."[3] Truly, Christianity in its purest and most powerful reality can be ours when we have a clear understanding of the Spirit's person and work. Whether we find ourselves exhilarated on mountain-top summits or in the shadows of daily struggle; whether in the quiet solitude of the countryside or the 24/7 noise of the city; whether in our private moments of intimate prayer or celebrating in gatherings of high-energy worship—the Holy Spirit is ready to conduct a Christ-exalting, supernatural work in your life starting today, and He will do it from the inside out.

"Since the Spirit of God was sent not only to be studied but ultimately to be experienced, it seems to me we have stopped short of God's intended purpose if we merely discuss and debate his presence instead of exulting in Him on an intimate basis." —CHARLES SWINDOLL

"There have always been people in the Christian Church who were very sure about the Holy Spirit. It was simple. He was the divine backer of their particular emphasis in theology and practice." —MICHAEL GREEN

AGREE TO EVALUATE YOUR ASSUMPTIONS

The Indwelling Spirit Challenges Me to Find the Balance of "Spirit and Truth"

P astor Jim Cymbala is well known for his book *Fresh Wind, Fresh Fire,* which has captivated and challenged thousands of readers with stories of dramatically changed lives. His wife, Carol, leads the famous Grammy-award-wining Brooklyn Tabernacle Choir. Cymbala preaches to over ten thousand every weekend in multiple church services. Every Tuesday night, thousands gather for the weekly prayer meeting, just as they have done for over forty years.

In recent years, Jim has become a treasured friend. He helps to lead a national coalition of pastors called *The 6:4 Fellowship* (64fellowship.com). Under this banner, Jim and I have sponsored one-day gatherings for Christian leaders in various cities across America, calling them back "to prayer and to the ministry of the word," the leadership priorities emphasized in Acts 6:4.

I've often heard Jim say, "When it comes to the Holy Spirit, churches are either cemeteries or insane asylums." Certainly there many churches that have found the balance and enjoy a rich experience of the Holy Spirit. But as I think of my own Christian journey, that pretty much sums it up. I was deeply embedded in and enamored with both extremes in the early years of my Christian faith, often bouncing between the two like a well-manipulated pinball.

DIVERSE AND DIVIDED

Looking back decades later, I am keenly aware of all the divergent opinions about matters of the Spirit. It seems so odd that the clear truth of the Scriptures about the person and work of the Holy Spirit has become so convoluted by our various doctrinal and denominational differences. The Spirit's work is to unite the people of Christ with one heart and mission. Somewhere along the way, we've mucked it up with debate, division, and even disdain.

It's quite difficult to be completely unbiased in our application of the doctrine of the Holy Spirit. We all suffer from some degree of subjectivity. I agree with David Peterson, who wrote, "Those who desire to bring their theology and practice under the criticism and control of the biblical revelation can find themselves in serious conflict with one another. Most of us are more conditioned by custom and personal preference in this matter than we would care to admit!"[1]

Some of us lack significant experience in the life of the Spirit and so tend to be very skeptical and even afraid of things outside our carefully defined practices. And some of us cherish certain experiences, some of which cannot be explained biblically, but are still very real. We can even make these experiences sacrosanct. This can create a filter through which we interpret the work of the Spirit and even judge others who have not been on the same journey.

I think it is safe to say that we have to get "past our past." This is not an easy or comfortable process. Yet it is absolutely essential if we are going to come to terms with clear New Testament experience of the Holy Spirit both personally and in our congregational gatherings. Reformed writer Michael Horton notes, "If some churches marginalize the Spirit in favor of the institution and its forms, others react simply by making the opposite choice. However, there are myriad ways of domesticating the Spirit besides assimilating his sovereign work to formalism. If some render the Spirit an ecclesiastical employee, others presume to make the Spirit a mascot for a movement or a prisoner of their own private experience."[2]

SPOOKED BY THE GHOST

According to research by the Barna Organization, most Christians do not believe that the Holy Spirit is a *living* force. (We'll talk more about the "force" word later.) "Overall, 38% strongly agreed and 20% agreed somewhat that the Holy Spirit is 'a symbol of God's power or presence but is not a living entity.'"[3] Among those who believe in the biblical understanding of the Holy Spirit, much confusion still exists.

The church I grew up in preached from the old King James Version of the Bible. In that translation, the Holy Spirit is called the "Holy Ghost." In my elementary years I would often watch a little cartoon titled "Casper the Friendly Ghost." It was not clear if this little guy was a boy who died and became a ghost or if he was just born to ghost parents. In any case, Casper was an outgoing goblin. Yet he often scared people in his attempts to befriend humans. One of his more popular lines stated, "I'll never be nothin' but a scary ol' ghost without any friends."

In my mind, I thought that maybe after Jesus died He came

back as the Holy Ghost. Like Casper, I assumed He was friendly, but I was a little bit spooked by the idea of a religious presence floating around waiting to show up at an unexpected moment to conduct some unusual spiritual business with me. Admittedly, this was beyond silly, but I wondered if the Spirit was also a bit scary to many other Christians and if they even really understood or embraced the whole idea of the Holy Spirit.

My childish misconceptions aside, I've met some Christians who seem to view the Holy Spirit as an ethereal, perhaps scary, entity hovering in the church's vent system, ready to pounce unexpectedly, inciting strange behaviors and out-of-the-box emotions—all for Jesus.

LEANING TOWARD THE SPIRIT

Depending on your upbringing (or religious television viewing habits), you may have witnessed some bizarre antics promoted to be church-as-usual. In my high-school years, I visited, witnessed, wondered and even tasted of a pretty titillating variety of Christian experiences attributed to the Holy Spirit.

Assembly of God scholar Gordon Fee admits, "Pentecostals, in spite of some of their excesses, are frequently praised for recapturing for the church her joyful radiance, missionary enthusiasm, and life in the Spirit. But they are at the same time noted for bad hermeneutics. . . . First, their attitude toward Scripture regularly has included a general disregard for a scientific exegesis and carefully thought-out hermeneutics (the science of the study of Scripture). In fact, hermeneutics has simply not been a Pentecostal thing. Scripture is the Word of God and is to be obeyed. In place of scientific hermeneutics, there developed a kind of pragmatic hermeneutics—obey what should be taken literally;

spiritualize, allegorize, or devotionalize the rest. . . . Secondly, it is probably fair—and important—to note that in general the Pentecostals' experience has preceded their hermeneutics. In a sense, the Pentecostal tends to exegete his experience."[4]

LEANING TOWARD THE TRUTH

At the more reserved end of the spectrum, many evangelical churches value heady, in-depth Bible teaching (and rightly so). Yet this mostly cognitive approach can inadvertently diminish a proper emphasis on the Holy Spirit. I will admit that for a season in my own life, I honestly viewed God as one big brain who worked exclusively in my mind. Anything below the neck might be excessive. I gave very little value to the total personality of the Spirit of God to work in my entire being—including my emotions (gasp!).

This cognitive bent can easily downgrade into a very predictable and systematized approach to the Christian life. I say it often: "Prayerlessness is my declaration of independence from God." The temptation to live on spiritual autopilot is constant. In our highly educated, prosperous, and theologically astute Christian cultures we can tend to settle for "zipper prayers" to open or close various gatherings.

Prayerlessness is my declaration of independence from God.

It also plays out corporately in the process of worship-planning and direction of worship services. The tech sheet is systematically concocted midweek, songs are plugged in, and the sermon is slotted like finely tuned machinery. Certainly, planning has its place. Yet, when a prayerful and substantive reliance on the Holy Spirit does not inspire and guide our planning, we stumble. When prayer is simply reduced to transition moments in the service, we are in danger of "doing church" week after predictable week, without a conscious and substantive reliance on the Holy Spirit.

In some circles, even biblical expressions of worship are frowned upon, such as joyful clapping or the lifting of hands in prayer and surrender. Anyone not aligning with a strict conservative view of the spiritual gifts is lumped in with extreme prosperity preachers. Lines are drawn. Camps are created. Disregard for anyone who disagrees tends to follow.

LEANING ON THE ATMOSPHERE

Most of my speaking opportunities in recent years have placed me in larger, typically nondenominational, congregations. These churches tend to have a sizable budget for their worship department. While participating in hundreds of these church services, I have observed that, in more recent years, the idea of experiencing the Holy Spirit is evidently associated with concert-style technology, digitized lights, environmental smoke, thundering sound systems, gargantuan images of worship leaders on a screen, and emotionally charged repetitive lyrics. While these tools are not necessarily wrong, they can become the perceived delivery systems of the presence of the Holy Spirit. And if one's church cannot provide enough of this spiritual oomph for an inspiring experience of God, you can always get tickets to an event where traveling Spirit-accelerating performers will really turbo-boost our encounter with "the presence." Ron Owens expresses his concern candidly: "Today, especially in the realm of church music, God is often being used to display man's talent rather than man's talent being used to display God."[5] Owens offers a heartfelt appeal:

> Be careful how you play with the emotions of the people God has entrusted to your leadership and care. Be careful that your people do not become so accustomed to getting a "praise high" when they come to church that a service seems empty if they do not experience it. Many today hop from group to group, from church to church, looking for higher highs. The tragedy is that they have been led to believe that what they are experiencing is the Holy Spirit, when it is nothing more than an intense emotional response.[6]

It's been said that what matters is not how high you jump on Sunday but how straight you walk on Monday. But ultimately, the devil's objective is not to diminish the excitement of our worship experience on weekends but rather, through any means, to discourage the empowerment of our daily walk in between. We have to make sure the sizzle of the service does not diminish the spiritual depth and enjoyment of our common walk with God.

We don't live at Disney World. While we all love extraordinary vacations, most of life is very mundane. As one friend says, "the work is in the valleys." The truth of

> **We have to make sure the sizzle of the service does not diminish the spiritual depth and enjoyment of our common walk with God. We don't live at Disney World. While we all love extraordinary vacations, most of life is very mundane.**

the indwelling Spirit of God can make the mundane meaningful and the ordinary extraordinary as we walk with Christ day by day. (Just in case you think that I am "against" emotions, chapter 9 of this book discusses how to enjoy the gift of emotion.)

LEANING ON OURSELVES

Regardless of your theological journey in connection to the Holy Spirit, you might need to overcome one other major factor in your past. I'll be the first to confess this one. We have a tendency to live independently of the Holy Spirit. We just don't sense a deep and consistent need for Him. My friend, Robbie Symons, summarized it well: "We need to stop trying and start relying!"

Charles Spurgeon, perhaps the greatest and most widely read preacher of recent centuries, exemplified a humble reliance on the Holy Spirit. His ministry, based at the Metropolitan Tabernacle in London in the late 1800s, resulted in scores of thousands of people coming to Christ along with the launching of an orphanage and a pastor's college. As he mounted the pulpit each week to preach to thousands, he silently declared to his own heart, with each of the fifteen steps, "I believe in the Holy Spirit. I believe in the Holy Spirit. I believe in the Holy Spirit." Spurgeon wrote: "Without the Spirit of God we can do nothing; we are as ships without wind, or chariots without steeds; like branches without sap, we are withered; like coals without fire, we are useless; as an offering without the sacrificial flame, we are unaccepted."[7]

PRYING US LOOSE

By now, I have probably emerged as an equal opportunity offender. Admittedly, I have spoken in broad terms around the categories of the spooky, the sensational, the stuck, the sizzling, and even the stubborn frameworks we adopt with regard to the work of the Spirit. But my heart's desire is to pry us all loose from anything that is not clearly biblical, spiritual, edifying, and gospel-promoting. These are urgent days in our society when the influence of the gospel is waning, to say the least. Our only real hope is Jesus Christ living through a revived church. This powerful enlivening work of the Word and Spirit must, in the truest sense, be an expression of the promises and principles of the Holy Spirit's own words, recorded in the Scriptures.

As we begin the journey together, I feel inadequate to write about the work of the Holy Spirit. I wonder if any writer is capable of dealing with so profound a theme. To borrow a common adage, "it is like trying to capture an ocean full of understanding in a thimbleful of thought." The person and work of the Holy Spirit is not always easy to define or explain. In the process of writing, I have read dozens of books, some of them quite peculiar and others far more in-depth and theologically rich than anything I could offer. I don't write because I am an expert or Pulitzer Prize– winning author. I write because truth has changed my life and is burning in my soul. I do not want to go to the grave before I share it in a way that will help the most people experience the best the Holy Spirit has to offer for the glory of Jesus and the supernatural advancement of His glorious gospel.

Still, I feel much like Warren Wiersbe when he wrote at the beginning of one of his (many) books: "I felt like a man trying to lay sunbeams in a row while evening was marching inexorably in. Then I decided that the problem was not the vastness of the subject but the narrowness of my own experience."[8]

OPEN MIND, OPEN HEART

Let's agree together that we want to embrace the best of both Word and Spirit. I urge you, at the points where you may disagree—ponder and explore with an open mind what the Bible actually teaches.

In his book *Forgotten God*, Francis Chan asks,

> Are you willing to pursue truth in your journey to know and be known by the Holy Spirit? Do you have enough humility to be open to the possibility that you have been wrong in your understanding of the Spirit? It's easy to get into "defensive mode," where you quickly disagree and turn to proof texts and learned arguments to defend what you've always believed. Rather than guarding your perspective, consider taking a fresh look at familiar passages to make sure you haven't missed something. You may end up with the same theology you've always had, but maybe you won't. Don't let your views be determined by a particular denomination or by what you've always been told. Within the context of relationship with other believers, seek out what God has said about His Spirit. Open up your mind and your life to the leading of the Spirit, regardless of what others may think or assume about you.[9]

Chan's words are important. Not only is the Holy Spirit often the "forgotten God," but for many of us He may be the "misrepresented God." Theologian Robert Lightner pointed out that the biblical doctrine of the Holy Spirit suffers today from three extremes: abuse, neglect, and distortion.[10]

I pray the Lord will give us discernment of those things really from Him. And, if we need to get past our past—then that's a great first step. For that to happen, we might need to loosen our grip on our tradi-

> **Not only is the Holy Spirit often the "forgotten God," but for many of us He may be the "misrepresented God."**

tions. Let's look honestly at our positions. Let's expose our experiences to the MRI of the Bible. And please, let this book drive you to the Scriptures as the divine teacher, the Holy Spirit, guides your thoughts and responses. Let's embrace these wise words from Andrew Murray:

> To everyone who honestly desires to know that he has the Spirit and to know Him in his person as a personal possession and teacher, we say: Study the teaching of the word in regard to the Spirit. Be not content with the teaching of the church or of men about the Spirit but go to the word. . . . Be determined to accept nothing but what the word teaches, but also to accept heartily all that it teaches.[11]

I trust you will feel a deep and lifelong conviction about your desperate need for the person and power of the Holy Spirit. Our Christian life is impossible without His indwelling presence. I pray that our heartfelt confession will habitually become, "I believe in the Holy Spirit. I believe in the Holy Spirit. I believe in the Holy Spirit."

"I looked at Christ and the dove of peace flew into my heart. I looked at the dove and it flew away." —ATTRIBUTED TO CHARLES SPURGEON

"When I see more talk than walk, more time given to money than the message, more jokes than Jesus . . . more hype than holiness, more about mantles than the Master, and more liberality with their morals than their miracles, then I have a right to be cautious, regardless of the miraculous." —DAVID RAVENHILL

EMBRACE THE HOLY SPIRIT'S PRIMARY PURPOSE

The Indwelling Spirit Inspires a Passion to Glorify Christ

Rick Warren's blockbuster book, *The Purpose Driven Life*, has sold over 30 million copies. Fans and critics alike admit the book struck a nerve in the human experience. Every breathing soul on earth longs to embrace a meaningful purpose in life. Purpose is the essential "why" that gives significance to all of the twists and turns, ups and downs, wins and losses of our journey. I remember hearing a college chapel speaker declare that you can tell a person *what* to do and they may attempt it for a season. But teach them *why* they are doing it and it will take a brick wall to stop them. Even Nietzsche, the pessimistic atheist philosopher was noted as saying, "He who has a why can bear almost any how."

THE PREEMINENCE OF PURPOSE

Foundationally, we can affirm the ultimate "why" of our very existence, and all things, is the glory of God. The Westminster Catechism states, "Man's chief end is to glorify God, and to enjoy him forever."[1] The purpose of the Father, Son and the Holy Spirit is united, clear, and eternal. All things are for the glory of God (1 Cor. 10:31).

I believe the primary thing that motivates God is His own glory. To our tiny minds, this may sound egotistical. But we must remember: God is the Creator and the One to whom all glory is due in the purity and beauty of His holiness.

During His earthly ministry, everything in the life of Jesus Christ, empowered by the Holy Spirit, was for the glory of the Father (John 11:4; 13:31–32; 17:1, 4–5). The ultimate result of God's salvation plan is that every knee should bow and every tongue should confess "that Jesus Christ is Lord, to *the glory of God* the father" (Phil. 2:10–11). Jesus came, lived, loved, served, sacrificed, died, and rose again—for God's glory.

WANTING THE WHY

In this book we are going to talk much about how the Holy Spirit works. Yet the most important issue in our understanding of the Holy Spirit is the *why,* the ultimate and guiding purpose, for which He was sent. God makes clear that He has a consistent and ultimate aim in all of the works of the Holy Spirit. This has to be our first and foremost point of common agreement, regardless of our backgrounds.

Jesus was not obscure about the "why" behind the impartation and indwelling of the Holy Spirit. He made it clear as to the reason it would be better for His followers that He ascended to heaven and, instead of His physical presence, impart the abiding Holy Spirit.

> "But when the Helper comes, whom I will send to you from the Father, the Spirit of truth, who proceeds from the Father, *he will bear witness about me.*" (John 15:26)

> "When the Spirit of truth comes, he will guide you into all the truth, for he will not speak on his own authority, but whatever he hears he will speak, and he will declare to you the things that are to come. *He will glorify me,* for he will take what is mine and declare it to you. All that the Father has is mine; therefore, I said that he will take what is mine and declare it to you." (John 16:13–15)

D. A. Carson elaborates: "Just as the Son by his ministry on earth brought glory to his Father ([John] 7:18; 17:4), so the *Paraclete* [Holy Spirit] by his ministry brings glory to Jesus."[2] A. B. Simpson, founder of the Christian Missionary Alliance denomination noted, "Let us not fail to grasp this precious truth that as Jesus Christ while on earth never did anything without the Holy Spirit, so now the Holy Spirit never does anything apart from Jesus."[3]

J. I. Packer offers two very helpful illustrations. The first is of a floodlight in a beautiful building, which does not exist for its own glory but to make clear and visible the splendor and wonder of its object by illumining its features. He also offers the illustration of a matchmaker ("the celestial marriage broker"), whose role is to bring us and Christ together and ensure we stay together.[4] In this way, the Holy Spirit glorifies Jesus according to the Word of God.

So the "why" behind the "who" and the "what" of the Holy Spirit is the glory of God through the magnification of Jesus, and the powerful proclamation of the gospel.

WHAT JESUS HAD IN HIS MIND AND HEART

When Jesus gave these words to His disciples in the upper room (recorded in John 13–16), He did so with full knowledge of what was before Him. He would soon face betrayal and brutal crucifixion. After His burial He would rise from the dead. He would appear to His disciples over a period of forty days then ascend to heaven, right before their eyes. Ten days later, on Pentecost, He would send the Holy Spirit to fill them and inaugurate His church. The Holy Spirit would empower this meager band of followers to boldly preach the gospel, give their lives for the cause, and eventually turn the world upside down.

Then in John 17 we see Jesus in prayer. In His extraordinary, intimate exchange with the Father we gain insight about what it would mean for them to be used by the Holy Spirit to testify of Him and bring Him glory.

JESUS' PURPOSEFUL PRAYER

An entire book could be written at this point on the prayer of John 17, but let's unpack a few key points.

Glory **is paramount.** Jesus was passionate about the glory of God: "Glorify your Son that the Son may glorify you" (v. 1). Jesus affirmed that He brought glory to the Father by accomplishing His earthly mission and also anticipated the restoration of His preincarnate glory after His return to heaven (vv. 4–5). He also spoke of the glory He would receive from the disciples (v. 10), and through them (v. 22). He even prayed for the day they would see His glory in heaven (v. 24). *True discipleship* is central. Prior to His ascension, Jesus' final commission would be for us to "make disciples of all nations" (Matt. 28:18–20). This John 17 prayer reflects all Jesus did to disciple these men. He gave them eternal life and the knowledge of the one true God (v. 2). He manifested God's name (character) to them (v. 6), teaching them to obey his truth (v. 6) that they might know the Father (v. 25). The core of His prayer reflects his longing for their protection, joy, and sanctification (vv. 11–19).

The *power of truth* is essential. Our Lord's prayer was peppered with references to truth, both in terms of the teaching Jesus had given them and regarding the power of truth in and through them (vv. 8, 14, 19). He prayed, "Sanctify them in the truth; your word is truth" (v. 17).

Unity is indispensable. Jesus prayed repeatedly for their unity in the gospel, "that they may all be one, just as you, Father, are in me, and I in you" (v. 21; see also vv. 11, 23). The Father's love in them would make this possible (v. 26).

The *global expansion of His kingdom* is the endgame. Jesus prayed for the advancement of the offer of eternal life through faith in Him. "So that the world may believe that you have sent me" (v. 21, see also vv. 23, 25). This gospel movement, soon to be birthed by the Holy Spirit, would bring salvation and ultimate transformation to the nations. No wonder Jesus spoke so clearly about the promise of His presence in and through them just before He prayed to the Father and prepared to send them as witnesses to the world.

Based on this overview of Jesus' prayer we can see that the Holy Spirit purposes to work in us to glorify Christ as we become disciples—and make disciples. The Spirit will work through the Word of the gospel to set us apart to Christ and to make us messengers of the truth. Christ is glorified when we are unified, at the deepest level, in His purposes, just as the Father and Son are one. And the Spirit uses us for Christ's glory as others believe through our proclamation of eternal life.

The book of Acts is a display of the answer to Jesus' prayer. We see the Spirit at work through the early church. Recently, while making my way through the book of Acts, as part of my daily Bible reading, I circled every mention of the Holy Spirit. You can certainly do this on your own, and ask the question, "How did the Holy Spirit work in this instance to glorify the person, work, and mission of Jesus?"

One thing is clear—the ultimate result of the work of the Holy Spirit is essentially the same: "He will glorify me ..." Instead of arguing our various viewpoints about *how* the Spirit works, as we so often do, let's seek resolute agreement on *why* the Spirit works. I believe this shared objective might minimize many of our secondary arguments. Even the arguments by their very nature can undermine the purpose of the Holy Spirit.

> **Instead of arguing our various viewpoints about *how* the Spirit works, as we so often do, let's seek resolute agreement on *why* the Spirit works.**

As Michael Horton has noted, "The apostles exhibited this Christ-centered focus in their sermons recorded in Acts and their use of the Old Testament in the epistles. In fact, the efficacy of the

Holy Spirit's mission is measured by the extent to which we are focused on Christ, 'the author and finisher of our faith' (Heb 12:2 KJV).... The Holy Spirit wants nothing to do with a Spirit-centered Christianity. It is therefore understandable that precisely because of his success, the Spirit's ministry in our lives would bring more attention to Christ than to himself."[5]

> **The Holy Spirit was given to glorify Jesus in our hearts, minds, and actions; in our homes and relationships; in our service, fellowship, and worship in His church.**

Let's keep the plumb line of God's purpose in mind. The Holy Spirit was given to glorify Jesus in our hearts, minds, and actions; in our homes and relationships; in our service, fellowship, and worship in His church. All this occurs as a witness to nonbelievers in our relational circle and beyond, into the near and far reaches of a lost world desperate to see and hear of our Christ.

Author Michael Green underscores: "The Spirit of Jesus points us back to Jesus. If we want to understand and possess the Spirit in his fullness, we need to keep our eyes firmly on Christ himself, for it is to him that all the Spirit's authentic witness is directed. If we do this we shall not claim as the teaching of the Spirit what does not relate to Jesus. And we shall not claim as experience of the Spirit what cannot be shown to flow from Jesus."[6]

HIS GLORY AND HIS TRUTH

Going back to Jesus' challenge in the upper room, we can't miss what He said in context about the direct means by which the Holy

Spirit would glorify Christ. How does the Holy Spirit glorify Christ? Let's look again carefully at the context of Jesus' words:

> "When the Spirit of truth comes, he will guide you into all the truth, for he will not speak on his own authority, but whatever he hears he will speak, and he will declare to you the things that are to come. He will glorify me, for he will take what is mine and declare it to you. All that the Father has is mine; therefore, I said that he will take what is mine and declare it to you." (John 16:13–15)

Notice several things. First, in this context, Jesus calls the *paraclete* the "Spirit of truth" who will guide us into all *truth*. This makes the communication of divine truth central to His purpose of glorifying Christ. As the Spirit of truth, He is the designated communicator of the heart, mind, truth, and will of the triune God. He speaks only what He hears in the counsels of the Trinity. He takes all Christ is, all Christ has done, and all Christ's purposes, and declares them to us. Theologian Boyd Hunt says it so well:

> The Spirit, then, is the *effective* actualizer of God's intentions. . . . Instead of the Spirit taking the place of an absent Father or Son, as is sometimes said, the Spirit effects Their presence and activity. Every filling of the Spirit is at the same time a renewed commitment to God's redemptive purpose in Christ. No New Testament principle is more essential than this to understanding of the Spirit's work.[7]

As Jesus said, the Spirit will take all that is His and make it real to us.

GOSPEL GLORY THROUGH US

We, too, are recipients of truth imparted by the Spirit. He gives us understanding and hunger to cherish the gospel as the object of our faith and the source of our fulfillment. As Paul wrote, "But far be it from me to boast except in the cross of our Lord Jesus Christ, by which the world has been crucified to me, and I to the world" (Gal. 6:14).

The Spirit conducts His teaching ministry by enabling us to understand, apply, and obey the Scriptures He inspired men to write. Jim Cymbala notes, "Our cravings for more of God's word aren't hunger pains we work up. A holy appetite grows inside of us through the work of the Holy Spirit that causes us to crave truth."[8] As Jesus said, "You search the Scriptures because you think that in them you have eternal life; and it is they that bear witness about me" (John 5:39). The Spirit takes the truth of God's Word that ultimately points to Jesus, and then we truly experience the truth that sets us free (John 8:32).

Paul explained that people who do not know Christ do not accept the things of the Spirit and consider them to be folly because they must be spiritually discerned (1 Cor. 1:18; 2:14). Yet of the believer Paul writes, "But, as it is written, 'What no eye has seen, nor ear heard, nor the heart of man imagined, what God has prepared for those who love him'—these things God has revealed to us through the Spirit. For the Spirit searches everything, even the depths of God" (1 Cor. 2:9–10). He goes on to explain that only the Spirit knows the deep things of God, but that we have received that Spirit so that we might understand the things freely given to us by God. And I love his compelling affirmation, "but we have the mind of Christ" (2:16).

So, with the mind of Christ, may we be ever mindful of the

glory of Christ. The book of Hebrews opens with these words: "In these last days he has spoken to us by his Son, whom he appointed the heir of all things, through whom also he created the world. He is the radiance of the glory of God and the exact imprint of his nature, and he upholds the universe by the word of his power. After making purification for sins, he sat down at the right hand of the Majesty on high" (Heb. 1:2–3). Yes, "All things were created through him and for him. And he is before all things . . . that in everything he might be preeminent" (Col. 1:16–18).

NOT TO US

One thing consistently undermines the Holy Spirit's chief purpose in our lives: self-glory. For many years I have been captivated by the passion of the psalmist: "Not to us, O LORD, not to us, but to your name give glory" (Ps. 115:1). It seems a lot easier for us to agree, "give Him the glory." It is another thing to sincerely feel and say, "Not to us." Perhaps that's why the psalmist repeated the phrase twice. Had I written that, I wonder if the Lord would have had me write it out ten times—or a hundred. "Not to me, O Lord!"

We all want the same thing: the full work of the Spirit. Yet His purpose is the glory of Christ. So to want the Spirit's fullness, and to be unaware of or unconcerned with our scramble for self-glory is a contradiction in no uncertain terms. The Spirit is not compatible with our personal or congregational ego inflations. Gordon Fee affirms, "The ultimate criterion for the Spirit's activity is the exaltation of Jesus as Lord. Whatever takes away from that, even if they be legitimate expressions of the Spirit, begins to move away from Christ to a more pagan fascination with spiritual activity as an end in itself."[9] Francis Chan concurs: "A sure sign of the Holy

Spirit's working is that Christ is magnified, not people. . . . The Spirit is here with us to accomplish God's purposes, not ours."[10]

In our day of on-demand viewing, social media, viral YouTube videos, and other endless avenues to showcase ourselves, we must be very clear about what a Spirit-directed, Spirit-controlled, Spirit-sensitive life does (and doesn't) look like. We must then be very discerning about what a real, Spirit-empowered gathering of Christians looks like. Regardless of the heightened levels of emotion, the dynamic persona of the preacher, the talent of the praise band, the contemporary design of the auditorium, the smooth execution of the service or any other attraction factors—there is one overruling cause. Is this about the glory of Jesus Christ? Is the objective crystal clear? Does it guide the elements of the service? Is it the real takeaway as people leave the campus? A. W. Tozer wrote, "The purpose of the Holy Spirit in the church is to glorify Jesus Christ, and he cannot be glorified when competing with celebrities and personalities."[11]

Paul captured the heart of a Spirit-filled believer, and the DNA of a Spirit-filled church, when he wrote that we are those who "worship by the Spirit of God and glory in Christ Jesus and put no confidence in the flesh" (Phil. 3:3). I truly believe the Holy Spirit makes it clear to our hearts when we drift into self-glory and are tipping too far toward efforts done in mere human strength and reason. I also believe He speaks to us when we are sitting in a worship service that is out of step with the Holy Spirit's sole purpose to glorify Christ.

WE WOULD SEE JESUS

At my ordination many years ago, I requested that a particular old hymn be sung. It is not hugely popular today, but I find the longing expressed in this song reflects what I hope will be the fruit of the Spirit's working in my life, and yours.

> *More about Jesus would I know,*
> *More of His grace to others show;*
> *More of His saving fullness see,*
> *More of His love who died for me.*

> *More about Jesus let me learn,*
> *More of His holy will discern;*
> *Spirit of God, my teacher be,*
> *Showing the things of Christ to me.*

> *More about Jesus, in His Word,*
> *Holding communion with my Lord;*
> *Hearing His voice in every line,*
> *Making each faithful saying mine.*

> *More about Jesus on His throne,*
> *Riches in glory all His own;*
> *More of His kingdom's sure increase;*
> *More of His coming, Prince of Peace.*

> *More, more about Jesus,*
> *More, more about Jesus;*
> *More of His saving fullness see,*
> *More of His love who died for me.*[12]

Yes! "Spirit of God, my teacher be, Showing the things of Christ to me." May the Spirit accomplish His purpose in our lives by empowering us to know more, think more, love more, cherish more, worship more, sing more, teach more, proclaim more—and make more—of the Lord Jesus Christ. Because the Holy Spirit is a purpose-driven Spirit.

"Instead of understanding the full benefits of the new covenant in Christ, most in the church live in a no-man's land between Jesus and Moses." —Jim Cymbala

"The new covenant comes with 'batteries included.' . . . The Spirit internalizes the New Covenant so that the people of God are motivated to do God's will." —Carl B. Hoch, Jr.

LIVE IN THE POWER OF THE NEW COVENANT

The Indwelling Spirit Radically Transforms the Way I Understand and See My Christian Life

C hanging leaves decorate the neighborhood. The summer breezes turn to chilling winds. Fall is in the air. Major League Baseball statistics dominate sporting news. Professional baseball playoffs have arrived.

Whether the lower tier perennial losers of the National League Central, the rebuilding club of the American League East, or last year's World Series champion—every team started the season with their eyes fixed on the same thing: The World Series ring. The gargantuan payoff. The Commissioner's trophy.

But only one team will finish the season on top. Maybe they escaped significant injuries. Perhaps they celebrated a late-inning, two-run RBI. No doubt, the right mix of personnel, a brilliant coach, and a winning game plan were core to their dominance. But not every team that wants the trophy gets the trophy.

As we continue in our quest for the best of the person and presence of the Holy Spirit, I reiterate: we all want the same thing. God's promises of the Sprit are sure and His power is real. But not all of us experience the fullness or maximum benefit of the Spirit in our lives. I propose that the new covenant is the watershed factor for our understanding of the power and practical implications of what the Bible describes as the work of the Holy Spirit.

REDISCOVERING A CORE INGREDIENT

Over the decades I have found great delight in verse-by-verse preaching. I heard it said once that the rationale behind this approach is that "God knows the needs of His people better than I do." I have also discovered, to my deep enrichment, that in teaching through books of the Bible, God also knows my needs better than I do. His Spirit powerfully addresses issues in my character as I preach systematically through His inspired Word, taking whatever passages might be next. This keeps me from just extrapolating repeatedly on the comfortable, familiar, borrowed, or "relevant" subjects. There is such power and applicability in the revealed order and meaning of the Spirit-imparted text.

During the most difficult days of my entire ministry, I was young, wounded, and disenchanted. Every fiber of my being wanted to walk away from pastoral service. My wife and I had already begun a process of finding a different career. But God, by His Spirit, intervened by restoring my perspective and realigning my understanding of the essence of Christian living.

In those months, the Lord had me teaching through the book of 2 Corinthians. This letter to Paul's "problem child" congregation has been noted as his most transparent. Because false teachers had infiltrated the church, Paul was forced to win the hearts of the Corinthians back to Christ, His gospel, and even to himself, the Lord's apostle. As the Holy Spirit inspired Paul to write, he also prompted Paul to open his heart with an authentic and even uncomfortable transparency. By so doing, we find in Paul's letter profound insight into the motivation and meaning of true gospel spirituality and ministry.

SALVAGED BY GOSPEL GLORY

I will confess that my study of 2 Corinthians was a powerful and timely tool of the Holy Spirit in salvaging my ministry and keeping me in the spiritual battle. At the core of this profound letter Paul talks about the true nature of his ministry (2 Cor. 2:14–4:8).

I needed this because, like most seminary grads, I had other superficial and diluted ideas about the nature of church work.

The centerpiece of Paul's understanding of ministry was found in his description of the power and superiority of the new covenant in contrast to the old covenant (3:1–4:7). Andrew Murray wrote, "The whole dispensation of the Spirit, the whole economy of grace in Christ Jesus, the whole of our spiritual life, the whole of the health and growth and strength of the Church, has been laid down and provided for, and secured in the New Covenant."[1] Murray gives us a prompt here as to why we need

> **To understand the impact of God's transforming presence we must have clarity and conviction to interpret our daily lives and our corporate worship by seeing through a distinctly new covenant lens.**

clear understanding about the meaning and application of the new covenant to our lives and our worship—even as Paul did.

At a personal level, my heart resonates with Murray when he writes, "All that God has ever done for His people in making a covenant was always to bring them to Himself as their chief, their only good, to teach them to trust in Him, to delight in Him, to be one with Him."[2] During my months of deep despondency as a pastor, God lavished these very blessings on me through my understanding of the new covenant. I was changed by what Paul described in these passages as I studied diligently and was empowered to preach passionately.

To understand the impact of God's transforming presence we must have clarity and conviction to interpret our daily lives and our corporate worship by seeing through a distinctly new covenant lens. D. A. Carson writes, "Christian worship is new covenant worship; it is gospel-inspired worship; it is Christ-centered worship; it is cross-focused worship."[3]

But what does this mean, and why does it matter?[4]

NEW COVENANT CLARIFICATION

The word "testament" and "covenant" are fundamentally the same word in the Hebrew and Greek. So in the simplest understanding, the Bible is divided between two covenants: the old covenant and the new covenant. The old covenant was enacted by God through the law and Moses. The new covenant was enacted by God through the person and work of Christ.

A covenant is defined as "a solemn commitment, guaranteeing promises or obligations undertaken by one or both parties, sealed with an oath."[5] Modern-day notions of a covenant are illustrated when nations form treaties, political systems ratify constitutions, businesses sign contracts, and when couples at the marriage altar make vows. Covenants in the Bible were sacred and serious, ratified by signs, solemn oaths, or even a meal. Sacrifice was often part of the process of ratifying a covenant. The term "cut a covenant" (Gen. 15:18 CEB) indicated the core component of blood sacrifice (Gen. 15:9–10, 17; Jer. 34:18).[6] One scholar explains that the blood sacrifice symbolized the "death" of the parties who were making the contract. It said that "thereafter in the matter involved, they would no more change their minds than can the dead."[7] Oath. Meal. Blood. No going back.

THE PRICE THAT BOUGHT PRIVILEGE

The dinner gathering was informal but rich with meaning. The men in the room had developed a profoundly deep connection in the recent years of working together. They were not just colleagues in a common cause but intimately connected friends. One of their company was about to die. They knew it. So this final meal held profound significance. Every bite savored. Every drink cherished. Every word weighty.

As He stared down His imminent death, the Host offered profound words of wisdom and encouragement to His associates. The entire evening led to one paramount moment.

Jesus took the bread and cup of the Passover meal and made a life-changing, yes, world-changing declaration. His words were measured. They captured the culmination of all that He had done, demonstrated, and declared. They framed the ultimate meaning of His death. They would shape the implications of His resurrection. They would offer a superior and powerful operating system to His future disciples for millennia to come. His pronouncement made the old religious structures and their vocabulary inferior in profound ways.

Paul summarized the momentous truths:

> For I received from the Lord what I also delivered to you, that the Lord Jesus on the night when he was betrayed took bread, and when he had given thanks, he broke it, and said, "This is my body, which is for you. Do this in remembrance of me." In the same way also he took the cup, after supper, saying, "This cup is the new covenant in my blood. Do this, as often as you drink it, in remembrance of me." For as often as you eat this bread and drink the cup, you proclaim the Lord's death until he comes. (1 Cor. 11:23–26; cf. Matt. 26:26–28; Mark 14:22–24; Luke 22:19–20)

Jesus spoke numerous times of His impending death, burial, and resurrection (Matt. 16:21; 17:22; Mark 8:31; 9:31; Luke 18:33; 24:7). In this final gathering He made it as clear as the noon day as to *how* God's loving plan of redemption was all going to come to fulfillment. Jesus introduced a new covenant that would supersede all that they had understood previously from their familiar Old Testament teaching. He would then proceed to elaborate in detail about the coming gift of the Holy Spirit, who would indwell them as the core empowerment for this new covenant.

When Jesus spoke of the sacrifice of His body and His own blood to seal a new kind of covenant, you can bet that the disciples had a sense of context from Old Testament teaching—and a heightened degree of concern about what they were hearing. Like firecrackers on the Fourth of July, their thoughts had to be exploding with the mixed emotions of impending loss and questions about the meaning of this new kind of covenant that would require their Teacher's blood.

Perhaps they remembered that this new covenant had been predicted by Ezekiel and Jeremiah:

> "And I will give you a new heart, and a new spirit I will put within you. And I will remove the heart of stone from your flesh and give you a heart of flesh. And I will put my Spirit within you, and cause you to walk in my statutes and be careful to obey my rules." (Ezek. 36:26–27)

> "Behold, the days are coming, declares the LORD, when I will make a new covenant with the house of Israel and the house of Judah, not like the covenant that I made with their fathers on the day when I took them by the hand to bring them out of the land of Egypt, my covenant that they broke, though I was their husband, declares the LORD. For this is the covenant that I will make with the house of Israel after those days, declares the LORD: I will put my law within them, and I will write it on their hearts. And I will be their God, and they shall be my people. And no longer shall each one teach his neighbor and each his brother, saying, 'Know the LORD,' for they shall all know me, from the least of them to the greatest, declares the LORD. For I will forgive their iniquity, and I will remember their sin no more." (Jer. 31:31–34)

Theologian Bruce Waltke illustrates the importance of the new covenant as seen in the Old Testament when he notes that the Holy Spirit is mentioned about seventy-eight times in the Old Testament, and about half of these refer to His new covenant ministries.[8] The Old Testament teachings had been pointing to this upper room moment for centuries.[9] The new covenant was God's plan from the beginning. It would replace the external and ritualistic systems of the old with spiritual and internal realities. It would refine and fulfill all God's promises in the old covenant.

> **We don't want our traditions, experiences, or current culture to derail us from the best and truest possibility of knowing a spiritually transforming worship life—weekly, daily, and moment by moment.**

As we reflect on this two thousand years later, we are overwhelmed in knowing that the possibility and privilege of living in the freedom of this new covenant came at a high price—the sacrifice of the life of the Son of God. This is one reason I want to be sure I get it right, sing it right, and say it right. This is why I have a burden to help you do the same.

Jesus made the essence of His covenant with us so clear, since He promised that the Holy Spirit would make it so possible, and since He gave His life for us to accomplish this. We don't want our traditions, experiences, or current culture to derail us from the best and truest possibility of knowing a spiritually transforming worship life—weekly, daily, and moment by moment.

NEW COVENANT APPLIED

Paul's elucidation of the contrast between the old and new covenants, specifically in 2 Corinthians 3:1–4:6, is one of the most helpful Paul ever wrote addressing the new covenant. It is also one of the most helpful applications of Jesus' upper room message that we find in the New Testament. Theologian Gordon Fee notes that this is the most significant passage on the work of the Holy Spirit in all of Paul's writings and the first time he has "set out in sharp contrast" the differences between the old and new covenants. He writes, "the argument from beginning to end has to do with the activity of the Spirit."[10]

In his teaching, Paul reflects back on the Old Testament law that came through Moses and even illustrates from Moses's profound experiences of the presence of God, as found in Exodus 34. In doing so, Paul may be countering some of the false teaching of those who were influencing the Corinthians. Yet for us, he creates a contrast that we must fully embrace to properly frame our life in Christ and our corporate worship. This chart provides a simple picture of what Paul explained in 2 Corinthians 3:1–16:

THE OLD COVENANT WAS:	THE NEW COVENANT IS:
Written with ink on tablets of stone (2 Cor. 3:3)	Written by the Spirit on our hearts (2 Cor. 3:2–3)
About the "letter" of the law that kills (3:6)	About the Spirit that gives life (3:6)
Marked by an external, temporary glory that has now faded (3:7-11)	Marked by a surpassing and permanent glory within us (3:7-11)
About the condemnation of sin (3:9)	About righteousness by the Spirit (3:8-9)
Shrouded by a veil of unbelief (3:12-16)	Marked by true freedom as the veil is removed by faith in Christ (3:14-16)

Paul's contrast here leads him to exclaim, "Now the Lord is the Spirit, and where the Spirit of the Lord is, there is freedom" (3:17). We have a liberating inside-out experience of the Spirit through the gospel. This is an application of what Jesus had declared, "And you will know the truth, and the truth will set you free. . . . So if the Son sets you free, you will be free indeed" (John 8:32, 36). Paul gave this reassurance, with a warning to the church at Galatia, "For freedom Christ has set us free; stand firm therefore, and do not submit again to a yoke of slavery" (Gal. 5:1). The new covenant has set us free from the ceremonies, restrictions, and limitations of the old. No turning back.

CAN'T MISS THIS!

So now let's go back to 2 Corinthians 3:18–4:7 to discover the profound application Paul offers as he unpacks a series of amazing truths. These are at the core of our new covenant experience of the Holy Spirit through the work of Christ.

Because this is so vital to our experience of the transforming presence of the Holy Spirit, I have placed the text here so you can read it carefully and prayerfully:

> Now the Lord is the Spirit, and where the Spirit of the Lord is, there is freedom. And we all, with unveiled face, beholding the glory of the Lord, are being transformed into the same image from one degree of glory to another. For this comes from the Lord who is the Spirit.
>
> Therefore, having this ministry by the mercy of God, we do not lose heart. But we have renounced disgraceful, underhanded ways. We refuse to practice cunning or to tamper

with God's word, but by the open statement of the truth we would commend ourselves to everyone's conscience in the sight of God. And even if our gospel is veiled, it is veiled to those who are perishing. In their case the god of this world has blinded the minds of the unbelievers, to keep them from seeing the light of the gospel of the glory of Christ, who is the image of God. For what we proclaim is not ourselves, but Jesus Christ as Lord, with ourselves as your servants for Jesus' sake. For God, who said, "Let light shine out of darkness," has shone in our hearts to give the light of the knowledge of the glory of God in the face of Jesus Christ.

But we have this treasure in jars of clay, to show that the surpassing power belongs to God and not to us. (2 Cor. 3:17–4:7)

Here are some compelling realities of the new covenant from this incredible passage:

- Every believer experiences freedom to be transformed into the likeness of Christ by the power of the indwelling Spirit, who is the Lord. He is God in us (3:17–18).

- We have the privilege of beholding the glory of Jesus Christ in face-to-face intimacy—a glory greater than what Moses experienced (3:18).

- We experience limitless power to become like Christ— "from glory to glory" (KJV) by the enabling of the indwelling Spirit who, again, is the Lord. Literally there is a *metamorphosis* that continues to change us (3:18).

- This transforming presence enables our gospel ministry and keeps us from losing heart (4:1).

- We are empowered to sincerely declare and live the truth of Christ in a way that deeply affects the conscience of the unbeliever (4:2).

- Our ministry to the spiritually blind involves a manifestation of the "light of the gospel of the glory of Christ." Christ is ministering in and through us by His indwelling presence (4:3–4).

- In keeping with the Spirit's sole purpose, we are empowered to die to self and declare Christ as Lord while living as humble servants. We decrease and Christ increases (4:5).

- God's power and light now reside in our hearts, making us agents of the "light of the knowledge of the glory of God in the face of Jesus Christ." Impact proceeds from intimacy (4:6).

- The indwelling treasure of the Spirit by the new covenant brings glory to God's surpassing power in us. There is no room for self-glory (4:7).

After applying these truths to his own life and hardships in ministry (2 Cor. 4:8–15), Paul gives this compelling statement: "So we do not lose heart. Though our outer self is wasting away, our inner self is being renewed day by day" (2 Cor. 4:16). The sustaining, renewing, continual sufficiency of the indwelling Spirit is our daily source of enduring faith and fruitfulness.

HEBREWS HITS HOME

The book of Hebrews, written to a persecuted, Jewish audience during the days of the early church, teaches extensively on the superior work of Jesus as our high priest and as mediator of the new covenant. The letter begins with this clear direction when it says:

> Long ago, at many times and in many ways, God spoke to our fathers by the prophets, but in these last days he has spoken to us by his Son, whom he appointed the heir of all things, through whom also he created the world. He is the radiance of the glory of God and the exact imprint of his nature, and he upholds the universe by the word of his power. After making purification for sins, he sat down at the right hand of the Majesty on high. (Heb. 1:1–3)

Space doesn't permit a full commentary on the profound teaching in this book about the superiority and impact of the new covenant, secured by the perfect sacrifice and present advocacy of Christ. Yet even a summary reading of Hebrews will flash some key truths like the burst of the sun's rising rays. Theologian Karl Hoch captures it well:

> The writer to the Hebrews has the new covenant in the back of his mind from the beginning to the end of his epistle . . . Christ has brought a better hope (7:19), a better covenant (7:22), better promises (8:6), better sacrifices (9:23), better possessions (10:34), a better homeland (11:16), better resurrection (11:35), and better blood (12:24). In so doing the author of Hebrews reminds his readers of the superiority

and finality of the new covenant over against the old covenant. Any retreat back to the old covenant is apostasy and will result in eternal loss.[11]

When Jesus cried out on the cross, "It is finished" (John 19:30), He meant it. He lived and died for this goal. The old covenant, initiated on Sinai, was fulfilled on Calvary. The new covenant had arrived. The promises, provision, and power of a new and living way had been accomplished in Jesus.

Like the wavering Hebrew believers, we can't go back to the old covenant and thus diminish the work of Christ or in any way dilute our faith in His sufficient work. We must live fully in the power and privileges of all that He has accomplished for us in the new, including our understanding of how His Spirit now works in our lives and in His church.

STUCK IN BETWEEN?

Jim Cymbala says, "In the New Testament we are breathing different air."[12] Indeed, we are—or at least we should be. Yet as I hear the common language of many of our conversations and Christian gatherings, I can't help but wonder if we are sincerely, but erroneously, seeking a new covenant experience with many leftovers of old covenant thought and language. We are suspended precariously with one foot on the dock of the Malachi and the other on the departing boat of Romans, and with some still confused about how to apply the space in between (the Gospels and the book of Acts).

In his book *Spirit Rising,* Cymbala points out the danger of living and teaching in a way that keeps us stuck in old covenant ideas while trying to live a new covenant life. He expresses great concern over popular teachers who "cherry pick" verses from the Old Testament, often out of context, without scrutinizing their teachings through the filter of the gospel. He targets prosperity preachers—but many of us who hold to pretty core evangelical beliefs can fall into the same trap in other ways.

Cymbala notes how important it is to distinguish between the old and new covenants. He writes, "The New Testament is our main guide for the age in which we live, and the Old Testament must be read in light of it." He continues, "Old Testament passages are only properly used when they ultimately point us to Jesus and the new covenant."[13]

J. I. Packer asserts "The right way for followers of Jesus Christ to read the Old Testament is in the light of all that was revealed in and through Christ and that now lies before us in the New Testament."[14] Clearly there is harmony between the Testaments. Christ is the fulfillment of both. His perfect sacrifice at Calvary and His Spirit in us is the power for us to fulfill the righteous requirement of God's moral law.

> **The new covenant supremacy matters because the finished work of Christ matters. A New Testament perspective on the work of the Holy Spirit matters because the words and work of Jesus matter.**

We are no longer stuck in old covenant practices or words in our understanding of Christ. I think of the disciples on the Road to Emmaus who encountered the risen Christ. "And beginning with Moses and all the Prophets, he interpreted to them in all the Scriptures the things concerning himself" (Luke 24:27). The new covenant supremacy matters because the finished work of Christ matters. A New Testament perspective on the work of the Holy Spirit matters because the words and work of Jesus matter.

As Carol Stockhausen has summarized, the difference between the old covenant and the new is the contrast of "something exterior versus something interior."[15] The gospel is truth that sets us free to experience all the benefits of life in Christ—specifically the transforming presence of the Holy Spirit who changes everything from the inside out (John 8:32; 2 Cor. 3:17). Chapter 10 will offer many practical applications of the transforming work of the indwelling Holy Spirit in your life.

So, like the thirty teams of Major League Baseball in pursuit of the World Series championship, we all want the same thing. In baseball, only one team wins the trophy. But in the Christian life, we can all attain the goal. In this season of your life and your church, let's understand and pursue the sure, scriptural, and specific pathway to victory called "The New Covenant."

Now, let's get specific as to what this new life journey should really look like.

"Renewed interest in the Spirit does not always mean clarity or consistency with respect to historic Christian teaching. It is not to be assumed that the Spirit whom people have in mind is the Spirit identified in Scripture." —MICHAEL HORTON

"If we think of the Holy Spirit as so many do as merely a power or influence, our constant thought will be, 'How can I get more of the Holy Spirit,' but if we think of him in the biblical way as a Divine Person, our thought will rather be, "How can the Holy Spirit have more of me?' The conception of the Holy Spirit as a divine influence or power that we are somehow to get a hold of and use, leads to self-exaltation and self-sufficiency. One who so thinks of the Holy Spirit and who at the same time imagines that he has received the Holy Spirit will almost inevitably be full of spiritual pride and strut about as if he belonged to some superior order of Christians." —R.A. TORREY

PURSUE THE INDWELLING PERSON, NOT AN EXTERNAL "PRESENCE"

The Indwelling Spirit Makes My Life in Christ Profoundly Personal

Over the years, various writers have imagined what the world might be like if Jesus had never come: a society without Christmas, Easter, or churches; Christian mission agencies, hospitals, orphanages, rescue missions, and ministries of various kinds would not exist. We would open a Bible that ended at Malachi. The promises of the gospel, the power of salvation, the expectation of resurrection, and hope of an eternal heaven would not be real to us. Our world would be dark, meaningless, and desperate beyond words.

Let's take that further and imagine what our lives would be like if Jesus had indeed come but had never sent the Holy Spirit. A. B. Simpson, founder of the Christian and Missionary Alliance, explains:

There could have been no Comforter and no comfort. The work which our Lord accomplished at so much cost could never have been completed. There could have been no conviction of sin, no repentance, no faith in the Lord Jesus Christ, no sense of forgiven sin, no balm of peace for the troubled conscience . . . no sanctification from the power of sin, no Spirit of intercession to help us and teach us to pray, no power to anoint us for our Christian work, no supernatural presence in our Christian life and in the life and work of the Church of God. All this would have been lacking if the Spirit had not come and our hearts would be orphaned indeed.[1]

Yet Jesus' promises were clear and His fulfillment of them sure. He told His disciples:

> "I will ask the Father, and He will give you another Helper, that He may be with you forever; that is the Spirit of truth, whom the world cannot receive, because it does not see Him or know Him, but you know Him because He abides with you and will be in you.
> "I will not leave you as orphans; I will come to you."
> (John 14:16–18)

Jesus' death was imminent as He spoke these words to His faithful band gathered in an upper room. His declared departure had to feel like the depressing headline of an impending tragedy. Surprisingly, Jesus told them that it was actually to their advantage that He would go away because, in doing so, He would then send them "the Helper" (John 16:7). Notice that Jesus spoke of the Spirit then said, "I will come to you." The Holy Spirit would be the very presence of Jesus in them. Pastor J. D. Greear commented, "Jesus claimed that having the Holy Spirit *in* them would be better than having him *beside* them."[2]

Soon, on the other side of the cross, the gift of the Holy Spirit would turn their physical loss into unimaginable triumph. They would not be alone. Jesus' final word of reassurance in His Great Commission assured, "I am with you always, to the end of the age" (Matt. 28:20). They knew, as we do, that He promised continued relationship with Him through the indwelling person of the Holy Spirit.

A RELATIONSHIP OF BELONGING

On a recent Sunday morning, outside an adult day care in a metropolitan Detroit neighborhood, a worker in that facility was drawn outside by what she thought was a crying cat. Instead, she found on the lawn a newborn baby, wrapped in a baby-blue blanket. The placenta and umbilical cord were still attached. Days later, as the infant was being cared for at a nearby hospital, authorities had been unable to identify the mother.[3]

Tragic scenes like this are repeated throughout the United States hundreds of times every year. The phenomena of "discarded infants" has become so widespread that all fifty states have enacted "Safe Haven" laws which decriminalize infant relinquishment under responsible circumstances, with the hope of saving the lives of innocent babies.[4] There are an estimated 153–210 million children around the world who have lost one or both parents. Millions more children have been abandoned or displaced, although exact numbers are unknown. Over 5,700 children are orphaned each day, and well over eight million children live in institutional care.[5] The calamity of abandoned children is beyond comprehension.

But we are not discarded infants. We are not orphaned children. Yes, we were at one time "children of wrath" (Eph. 2:3), "separated from Christ," alienated from His family, strangers to His promises, "having no hope and without God in the world" (Eph. 2:12). We were enslaved to another master—sin (Rom. 6:17).

But our redemption and adoption has delivered us from our former father—the devil (John 8:44). The New Testament describes this so powerfully:

> For you did not receive the spirit of slavery to fall back into fear, but you have received the Spirit of adoption as sons, by whom we cry, "Abba! Father!" The Spirit himself bears witness with our spirit that we are children of God. (Rom. 8:15–16)

> And because you are sons, God has sent the Spirit of his Son into our hearts, crying, "Abba! Father!" (Gal. 4:6)

The Aramaic term *Abba* was a term in Jesus' day used by a child who was in personal, assured, intimate fellowship with this father. It was a term Jesus used in speaking to the Father (Mark 14:36). John Piper comments, "God does not leave us in the condition of aliens when he adopts us. He does not leave us with no feelings of acceptance and love. Rather, he pours his Spirit into our hearts to give us the experience of being embraced in the family. . . . Therefore, in adopting us, God gives us the very Spirit of his Son and grants us to feel the affections of belonging to the very family of God."[6]

Not only is the adoption metaphor one of the compelling themes of the New Testament, but it is also a truth that helps us understand that the Holy Spirit's work in us is ultimately personal.

What idea could more powerfully reflect a merciful, loving, secure and intimate *relationship* than adoption? The relational aspect of our life in Christ is deeply rooted in a vital truth: the Spirit is a person, abiding, working, and living through us.

NOT A FORCE!

As I have traveled the nation, speaking in a wide assortment of congregations, I have observed a troubling trend of language that depersonalizes the Holy Spirit. Rather than the indwelling, supernatural, and personal indwelling of God's Spirit, the language of songs, and even preachers, might lead many to believe that the Holy Spirit is some ethereal "force" that periodically appears, perhaps blowing in from the building's ventilation system. I get the feeling in many places that we are conjuring up an elusive "it" rather than celebrating and cherishing the transforming power of an indwelling "Him."

> **I get the feeling in many places that we are conjuring up an elusive "it" rather than celebrating and cherishing the transforming power of an indwelling "Him."**

According to a recent study by LifeWay Research, 56 percent of evangelical Christians say the Holy Spirit is a force rather than a person. In that same study, a quarter (28 percent) said the Spirit is a divine being but not equal to God the Father and Jesus. Half (51 percent) disagreed, and 21 percent were not sure.[7] I am convinced that even among those who intellectually and theologically affirm that the Holy Spirit is a person, many still speak of Him as a "force" that paranormally arrives from some other location. Many who intellectually believe the Holy Spirit is a person still sing and speak about Him as if He were a force. They describe Him in obscure third-person language as "The Presence" or a "power" in the atmosphere. I am deeply concerned that the Holy Spirit, even in contexts where His work is emphasized and His presence evoked, has become the "misrepresented God."

Francis Chan agrees: "He is not an indistinct 'power' or 'thing.' I often hear people refer to the Spirit as an 'it,' as if the Spirit is a thing or force that we can control or use. This distinction may seem subtle or trivial, but is actually a very serious misunderstanding of the Spirit and His role in our lives."[8]

We will be more specific and practical about this in later chapters but for now let me emphasize that while this may be well-meaning, it detracts from the great New Testament reality of the person of the Spirit *dwelling within* us. This can subtly diminish our conscious, moment-by-moment enjoyment and consistent empowerment by the indwelling Christ. Most troubling, a confused view of the Holy Spirit can distort the sufficiency of our promised new covenant experience based on the glorious person, sufficient work, and clear promises of Jesus Christ.

THE POWER OF PERSONHOOD

In the next few pages we are going to emphasize the personal character of the Holy Spirit. Of course, this in no way diminishes His absolute deity. The Spirit is holy, indicating He is God. Jesus declared that the "name" (singular in the Greek) by which we are to be baptized is "of the Father and of the Son and of the Holy Spirit" (Matt. 28:19). I love the summary given at the beginning of the updated Westminster Confession: "The Holy Spirit, the third person in the Trinity, proceeding from the Father and the Son, of the same substance and equal in power and glory, is, together with the Father and the Son, to be believed in, loved, obeyed, and worshiped throughout all ages."[9]

The Holy Spirit is also symbolized in some important *impersonal* terms to help us understand how He works. He is described in the New Testament as:

THE HOLY SPIRIT IN THE NEW TESTAMENT		
Symbol	**Scriptures**	**Significance**
Wind	John 3:8; Acts 2:2	Helping us understand the invisible, uncontainable, and powerful work of the Holy Spirit.
Fire	Matthew 3:11; Acts 2:3	Indicating God's holy presence and purifying power.
Oil	Luke 4:18; Acts 10:38; 1 John 2:20	A symbol of the Holy Spirit's empowerment, understanding, and healing in our lives.
Water	John 7:37–39	Symbolizing the Spirit's work in refreshing, cleansing, and renewing us.
Dove	Luke 3:22	Representing the Holy Spirit's gentle, peaceful dealing with our lives through Christ.
Earnest/Seal	2 Corinthians 1:22; 5:5; Ephesians 1:13–14; 4:30	Assuring us that the Spirit is God's pledge or down payment toward our final glorification with Christ.

First fruits	Romans 8:23	An indicator of the coming harvest of salvation and glory for the believer.
Seven	Revelation 1:4, 5	A numeric symbolism of completion indicating the fullness and sufficiency of His power and work.

THIS IS PERSONAL

In his book *The Names of the Holy Spirit*, Elmer Towns proposes that Jesus' favorite name for the Holy Spirit is *paraclete* because it was the name He used repeatedly in His intimate description of the Spirit to His disciples in the upper room.[10] In that final gathering He used this name four times (John 14:16, 26; 15:26; 16:7).[11] *Paraclete* is rooted in the compound verb in the Greek with the prefix *para*, meaning "alongside" and the verb *kaleo*, "to call." It can be understood as a "strengthener, helper, comforter, advocate, supporter, advisor, ally or senior friend" who is called alongside. Jesus promised this personal expression of His own presence would be *in* them (John 14:16). This description announces "personal relationship" like a gargantuan, radiant billboard on Broadway.

Using some simple (and woefully inadequate!) human comparisons to illustrate the vast and personal nature of the ministry of the Holy Spirit in our lives, let me describe Him this way:

- Like a truly authentic, transparent and always faithful *friend*, He wants us to know Him and pledges to be with us without recourse (John 14:26).

- Like an all-wise *instructor*, He teaches us and reminds us of the things of Christ (John 15:26).
- Like a perfect *judge* and forceful *attorney*, He convicts hearts of sin, righteousness, and judgment (John 16:8–11).
- Like an experienced *guide*, He shows us the way of truth both in the present and for the future (John 16:13; Rom. 8:14).
- Like a powerful and courageous *preacher*, He witnesses of Christ both to and through us (Acts 1:8; 2:4; 4:8; 5:32).
- Like an all-knowing *mentor*, He speaks clearly to us to showing us His will, His calling, His direction, and His redirection (Acts 13:2; 16:6–7).
- Like a reassuring *older sibling*, He gives clear personal assurance that we are truly sons of God (Rom. 8:16).
- Like a seasoned, godly *saint*, He understands our inadequacy, showing us how to pray from deep within our hearts, sometimes beyond our ability to even articulate those Spirit-given thoughts (Rom. 8:26).
- Like an exceedingly generous and perfect *benefactor*, He imparts to each of us supernatural gifts that we might steward those blessings to selflessly serve and build up one another (1 Cor. 12:7–11).
- Like a patient, preserving, and godly *parent*, He shows us how to walk (live) so that we overcome the destructive powers of the flesh while journeying in an evil world (Gal. 5:16–18).
- Like the gentle voice of a caring *parent* or the warning shout of a *lifeguard*, He speaks to us collectively, calling us to repentance, renewal, and restoration (Rev. 2:7, 11, 17, 29; 3:6, 13, 22).

As the ultimate example and expression of Christlikeness, He produces His very character of "love, joy, peace, patience, kindness, goodness, faithfulness, gentleness, self-control" in us. Notice these are all very personal and relational qualities (Gal. 5:22–23). The New Testament tells us that the Holy Spirit can be "lied to" (Acts 5:3–4). He can be "grieve[d]" (caused to feel sorrow or distress) by our disobedience or neglect (Eph. 4:30). Gordon Fee summarizes, "this is the language of personhood, not that of an impersonal influence or power."[12] A. H. Strong says it this way: "That which searches, knows, speaks, testifies, reveals, convinces, commands, strives, moves, helps, guides, creates, recreates, sanctifies, inspires, makes intercession, orders the affairs of the church, performs miracles, raises the dead—cannot be a mere power, influence, efflux, or attribute of God, but must be a person."[13]

KNOWN, LOVED, WORSHIPED

Because the Holy Spirit is a person, He is to be intimately known, deeply loved, and clearly understood. Because He is God, we relate to Him in abandoned worship, unquestioned obedience, and full surrender.

Practically speaking, I love the way one Puritan writer from the 1600s stated it: "Our worship is sometimes with the Father and then with the Son, and then with the Spirit. Sometimes the believer's heart is drawn out to consider the Father's love in choosing, and then the love of the Son in redeeming. And sometimes His heart is drawn to the love of the Holy Spirit that searches the deep things of God and reveals them to us. . . . We should never be satisfied with our worship until all three persons lie level in us and we sit in the middle of them while they all manifest their love to us."[14]

If He were simply a force we summon, then He could be reduced to an "object" that we use for our temporal purposes and personal desires. Few things could be more contrary and offensive to the One whose holy presence is meant to rule and transform us. Nothing could more seriously contradict the finished work of Christ and His beautiful plan for this new kind of relationship, for which He shed His blood. Nothing could more seriously undermine our holy and beautiful relationship as adopted children brought into an assured and holy "belonging" to a loving Lord and Savior.

Boyd Hunt summarized it well: "Most importantly, the Holy Spirit, who is personal, acts personally, not impersonally or magically. Those who view the Holy Spirit as an impersonal power are concerned about how to control or use Him. By viewing the Spirit personally, as the Spirit of the God we know in Christ, our concern should be to let the Spirit control our lives."[15] And, I would add, what beautiful, profound and ultimately fulfilling control this can be!

THE SPIRIT OF CHRIST

None of us would think of Christ as an "it" or some amorphous presence floating just below the ceiling of the worship center. We think of Jesus in very personal terms springing from all of the compelling pictures of His life as seen in the Gospels. We picture His love, compassion, mercy, confrontation of sin, and very intimate relationships with His followers. While Jesus and the Spirit are distinct in personality, the New Testament still describes God's presence in us as "the Spirit of Christ" or "Christ in you" (Rom. 8:9–11; see also Phil. 1:19; Gal. 4:6; Eph. 3:16–17; Gal. 2:20; Col. 1:27). So, to be accurate in our relationship with the Holy Spirit, we must think of Him as the indwelling presence of an intimate Savior, Lord, and Friend. Gordon Fee notes, "The Spirit's agency can hardly be less personal than that of Christ."[16]

It's been said that Jesus puts a face on the Holy Spirit. I like that. British scholar James D. G. Dunn elaborates in describing the New Testament work of the Holy Spirit: "Vitality of the Christian experience does not cease because the historical Jesus has faded into the past and the coming of Jesus has faded into the future; it retains its vitality because the Spirit is at work here and now as the other Paraclete."[17]

> The more stimulating the technology, the more aggressive we must be in emphasizing the inside-out work of the indwelling Spirit over any outside-in persuasion of the senses that can be prompted by the tools of the worship experience.

We cannot think of the Holy Spirit in impersonal terms. His "presence" is not some mystical gas or the arrival of some nondescript energy force. His presence is very personal. He lives in us personally. He works in us personally. He moves in and among us personally.

I've been to some churches that I think should be called "Star Wars Community Church" because much of how they sing and speak leave me with a salient message: "The force is with you." When you add the environmental smoke, digital lights, massive amplification (and even some sound effects), I'm ready to pull out my light saber and take on Darth Vader. Or maybe it's supposed to be the devil. Who knows?

Let's be honest: the more externally stimulating our worship has become the harder it seems for us to focus on the internal work of the Holy Spirit. As I will note in chapter 8, there is nothing inherently wrong with our high-tech tools as long as we use them with a clear objective and not allow them to blur our biblical purpose. The glory of Christ is best facilitated, and the work of the Holy Spirit best communicated, when we teach clearly and reiterate regularly the truth of the *indwelling* Spirit, not some "surrounding" presence that becomes associated with the tools themselves. I would suggest that the more stimulating the technology, the more aggressive we must be in emphasizing the inside-out work of the indwelling Spirit over any outside-in persuasion of the senses that can be prompted by the tools of the worship experience.

It is helpful for us to reflect on early New Testament worship. Instead of people scoping out the latest clothing styles, they gathered wearing very simple robes. The rooms were basic—typically a modest home. Lighting options were twofold: sunlight or oil lamps. The music was very organic; either a cappella or with minimal instruments. "Church" was not focused on where the people gathered but *that* the people gathered. There's was a simple, pure, spiritually extraordinary community. The work of the Holy Spirit was their only source of all good things. His indwelling was forefront in their minds, cherished in their hearts, and celebrated in their midst.

ALL PRESENT, STILL PERSONAL

But isn't the Holy Spirit also omnipresent? Yes. Of course, the doctrine of the omnipresence of the Spirit is intricately connected to His deity. There is no place where any person of the Trinity is ever absent. This is hard for us to grasp, but it is clearly taught in the Bible. One writer explains,

> If we could fully grasp the concept of eternity, the omnipres-
> ence of God might be within our comprehension. The
> human mind classifies events along a sequential timeline,
> with specific divisions for the past, present, and future. . . .
> Since God is eternal, spatial dimensions cannot restrict
> Him. God's time is infinite; therefore, God is also unre-
> stricted with respect to space. . . .
> . . . the omnipresence of God confirms that God con-
> tinually looks upon mankind.[18]

The standout passage that teaches the omnipresence of God's
Spirit is found in Psalm 139, where David writes of the assurance
of the presence of the Spirit in every place. Yet even in this landmark psalm, the bottom-line application of the omnipresence of
the Spirit is focused on the heart. The psalm begins and ends, not
with a focus on a mystical manifestation but rather the Spirit's
primary concern with the heart. The psalm opens, "O LORD, you
have searched me and known me!" (v. 1) and closes with "Search
me, O God, and know my heart! Try me and know my thoughts!
And see if there be any grievous way in me, and lead me in the way
everlasting!" (vv. 23–24). Puritan John Owen wrote,

> The presence of the Holy Spirit everywhere and in all things
> is not the same thing as his personal indwelling in believers.
> As God, one in the same being in substance with the Father
> and the Son, he fills all things and is everywhere present but
> his indwelling is personal, belongs distinctly to him as the
> Spirit of God and is voluntary. It wholly depends on a free
> act of his will. . . . He is essentially everywhere and can work

where and how he pleases without indwelling any person. What is promised to believers is the Spirit himself and his coming to live in them in a special way: "He will be in you."[19]

Our obligation as disciples, and our privilege under the new covenant, is to fully embrace and experience the promise of His indwelling. God's concern is not that we would search for His elusive presence in the atmosphere or in the sea or in the desert. His purpose was that we would acknowledge His ever-present desire for an intimate relationship with His children, a relationship that ultimately ministers to and changes their hearts.

As I noted in an earlier chapter, a failure to think of the Holy Spirit in personal terms, coupled with a lack of emphasis on the paramount gospel teaching of His indwelling in our hearts, has created a mountain of mental mush about what we mean when we speak of His presence. We need a clear new covenant understanding of how the Holy Spirit works in our lives and in the church today.

PERSONAL ON PURPOSE

One of the more inspiring stories of our time, made prominent by the movie *The Blind Side*, captured millions of hearts with the account of Michael Oher, a homeless teen from Memphis. He had drifted in and out of the school system for years. Feeling a special affection for Michael, Leigh Anne Tuohy and her husband took him in, eventually becoming his legal guardians. They had a clear purpose—they did everything possible to help him achieve his incredible potential as an athlete. This required rigid discipline, family structure, relentless academic tutoring from Miss Sue, and massive amounts of loving encouragement in the context of a determined personal relationship. Their intentions for Michael transformed his life—and theirs. He emerged as a formidable force on the gridiron and has become one of the best offensive tackles in the NFL.

The Father has adopted us, in Christ, and placed His Spirit in us. Galatians 4:6 affirms our relationship, "And because you are sons, God has sent the Spirit of his Son into our hearts, crying, 'Abba! Father!'"

Yes, we are loved. We belong to Him. We are not alone. He is not a distant or unexplainable force. His personal power and presence pulsates in and through our lives. But just as the Tuohy's had a purpose for Michael Oher, and just as Miss Sue enabled him to excel, so God has a very specific purpose for every aspect of our experience of His Holy Spirit. The Spirit in us is our permanent 24/7 loving, indwelling coach and tutor—to empower us to glorify Christ (just in case you forgot the "why" behind all that He does).

"Worship is not restricted to what we do when we come together in church, but about the way we relate to God through the Spirit and in accordance with the teaching of Jesus, and that touches the whole of life." —COLIN G. KRUSE

"'Within you! Within you!' . . . God created man's heart for His dwelling. . . . 'the kingdom of God is *within you*.' It is *within* we must look for the fulfillment of the new covenant. . . . The Spirit of Christ himself is to be within us as the power of our life. Not only on Calvary, or in the resurrection, or on the throne is the glory of Christ the conqueror to be seen—but in our heart. *Within* us is to be the true display of the reality and the glory of His redemption. Within us, in our inmost parts, is the hidden sanctuary where the ark of the covenant is sprinkled with blood. It contains the law written in an ever-living writing by the indwelling Spirit, and where, through the Spirit, the Father and the Son now come to dwell." —ANDREW MURRAY

WORSHIP LIKE *YOU* ARE THE "HOUSE OF THE LORD"

The Indwelling Spirit Empowers Me to Worship as the Church, Not Just at Church

The adult grandchildren did well in business. From their personal savings and profitable returns in multiple investments they enacted a wonderful plan to bless a treasured family member. Grandma Louise ranked at the top of their list of the loved and admired. Since Grandpa's death six years ago she survived on a paltry Social Security stipend. Her threadbare furniture reflected the styles of the '80s. Her décor was outdated and dilapidated. Chronically deferred maintenance made the place almost unlivable.

The day came when the family surprised Louise with a brand new home. A gift of deepest love and care for their beloved family matriarch. Stunned at the modern functionality, cleanliness and convenient layout of the brand-new home, she was speechless. As she settled into her new digs during the following weeks, she was not sure what to think. The grandkids would hang on to her old home long enough to relocate her furnishings and refurbish the out-of-date place. Then the plan was to put it on the market at a reasonable price.

A week later, Tommy, the oldest of the grandchildren and primary investor in the new residence, stopped by to visit Grandma. To his dismay, she was not home. Immediately, he called her cell phone only to discover that she had settled back into the timeworn house. She just could not seem to shake her emotional attachment to the derelict old place.

Like Grandma Louise, we can tend to go back to the old ways when we think about the "house of the Lord." This reversal to an inferior dwelling place of God's Spirit might be keeping us from a full experience of the new covenant promises and privileges as the very dwelling place of the Spirit of God.

Over my decades of ministry, I've had misgivings about a very common phrase used to greet church attendees. You'll hear it often: "Welcome to the house of the Lord!" This sincere expression can be interpreted in a variety of ways. My hope has been that it is understood as a reference to the gathering of the people, irrespective of a facility. My fear is that we are perpetuating another holdover idea from the old covenant, that the physical building is some sort of sacred temple. My core concern is that casual expressions like this one, without a clarification about the inside-out work of the Holy Spirit, could be diminishing our experience of true new covenant worship.

The "Lord's house" is ultimately the *people*, not the *building*. The use of a Christian building may be sacred for sure, but the essence of the building is . . . well, just a building. Many Christians can be like Grandma Louise—stuck in the old place, under the impression that "the church" is ultimately an immobile building or structure rather than the people, and unaware of the sacrifice and love that has provided something far superior.

A NEW REALITY OF WORSHIP

John 4 contains a landmark story in Jesus' ministry that shows His compassion for outcasts. As a Jewish man, He does the unthinkable by engaging a Samaritan woman in heartfelt conversation. Standing beside Jacob's well, He takes the occasion of His own thirst to actually offer her His heart-transforming living water. In the interchange, He demonstrates His transcendence over cultural, gender, racial, and religious barriers.

As the conversation unfolds, He exposes her spiritual thirst and reveals His supernatural knowledge of the unsavory details of her life. She soon realizes this is no ordinary man, and she initiates dialogue about the religious differences between Jews and Samaritans. "The woman said to him, 'Sir, I perceive that you are a prophet. Our fathers worshiped on this mountain, but you say that in Jerusalem is the place where people ought to worship'" (John 4:19–20). The Samaritans had built their temple on nearby Mt. Gerizim, in view from where Jesus and the woman were standing. The Jews held Jerusalem and the Old Testament temple located there as being sacred.

Jesus steps through this conversational open door with teaching that set the course for a brand-new reality of worship, based in the work of the gospel—a gospel embodied and delivered by Him. Jesus said to her,

> "Woman, believe me, the hour is coming when neither on this mountain nor in Jerusalem will you worship the Father. You worship what you do not know; we worship what we

know, for salvation is from the Jews. But the hour is coming, and is now here, when the true worshipers will worship the Father in spirit and truth, for the Father is seeking such people to worship him. God is spirit, and those who worship him must worship in spirit and truth." (John 4:21–24)

Jesus describes the "hour" of His death on the cross, His burial, His resurrection, and His sending of the Holy Spirit (see also John 2:4). He underscores this again in verse 23, speaking of the hour that was coming (His future work) and is "now here" (in His present ministry). So, in light of His gospel mission, He makes clear that true worship is not rooted in a physical location or focused around a man-made structure. D. A. Carson writes,

> This worship can take place only in and through him: he is the true temple (2:19–22), he is the resurrection and the life (11:25). The passion and exaltation of Jesus constitute the turning point upon which the gift of the Holy Spirit depends (7:38–39; 16:7); but that salvation-historical turning point is possible only because of who Jesus is. Precisely for that reason, the hour is not only "coming" but also "has now come."[1]

And now, He gives the new reality. Those of us on this side of the cross understand it as the worship reality of the new covenant (as we saw in chapter 3).

Jesus clarifies the nature of "true" worship that is based on His person and work. The Greek word for "true" means real and genuine, pointing forward to the worship made possible by the gospel and experienced through the indwelling Holy Spirit.

No doubt, temple worship for the Jews had a beauty of its own. The Psalms contain some wonderful accounts of God's people experiencing Him in worship with choirs, instruments, and heartfelt prayers. I think of Psalms 42, 43, 84 and others that speak of experiencing God's presence in their designated place of worship. I love praying from the Psalms on a regular basis. But Jesus changed everything.

THE WORSHIP HE WANTS

Have you ever wondered, "What does God want me to experience in worship?" Not what does my church want, not what do the worship leaders promote, not what is popular right now—but what does God really want? Well, here Jesus describes the very worship the Father seeks, desires, and blesses. This worship is based on the truth that God is "spirit," which (as Jesus repeats twice) defines true worship. The phrase "God is spirit" is an insight into how He relates to us as an invisible and transcendent God. This is all about God's "mode of action and working."[2] *Spirit* in the Bible "is the life-giving breath of God, which quickens and illumines the hearts and minds of men."[3] David Peterson writes, "'Spirit' and 'truth' are God's gifts through Jesus, by which he sustains us in genuine relationship with himself."[4]

Is this your focus and experience in worship? Gospel worship is a spiritual work, not something primarily conducted through buildings, sound systems, high-tech lighting, or other forms that we might attach to what we call "worship" in our modern framework. As D. A. Carson says, "He cannot be domesticated by mere location or mere temples, even if in the past he chose to disclose himself in one such temple as a teaching device that anticipated what was coming."[5]

William Barclay says it clearly, "If God is spirit, God is not confined to *things*." He points out that worship focused on

physical objects is tantamount to idol worship and is not only ir-
relevant but an insult to the very nature of God. He also notes that
"God is not confined to *places*" and to limit the worship of God to
a location puts a limit on real worship "which by its nature over-
passes all limits."[6] Our modern-day reliance on "things," whether
it be traditional forms or high-tech devices, potentially puts us
in a place of spiritual diversion. None of us wants to be led away
from the biblical reality God desires.

SPIRIT *AND* TRUTH

Jesus is telling this woman, and us, that true worship is experienced in "spirit and in truth." Commentators debate as to whether
Jesus is referring to the human *spirit* or the Holy *Spirit*. My answer
is "yes." Only a Spirit-transformed life can worship from his spirit.
As Jesus said to Nicodemus in the previous chapter, "That which
is born of the flesh is flesh, and that which is born of the Spirit is
spirit. Do not marvel that I said to you, 'You must be born again'"
(John 3:6–7).

To worship "in spirit and truth" is not about two different
components. We don't worship in spirit when we are singing with
raised hands then later worship in truth when we are listening to
the sermon. This true worship is one intimate, all-in experience.
Christopher Ash writes, "You cannot measure Bible and the Spirit
against one another. You cannot set Bible and Spirit side-by-side
and say we need more of one and less of the other."[7]

From Jesus' words we realize real worship is not just something we do in a church building. Certainly, the facilities and instruments of worship, when properly understood, can accommo-
date worship. But real worship is the lifestyle and passion of a true
Christian 24/7. This is worship that is empowered by the Holy

Spirit at the deepest level of our humanity. Worship is enlightened by the revelation of the One who is the truth (John 14:6) and whose life in us is the "Spirit of truth" (John 14:17; 15:26).

We often speak of our gatherings as an "encounter" with God. For years, I even led a weekly prayer service at our church called "Fresh Encounter" and have a book titled *Fresh Encounters.*[8] Often as people gather to pray at the building on a Sunday morning I hear them say, "Thank you Lord that we can come into Your presence today." I'm not sure if they are still stuck in the old covenant "building mode" or truly thinking of the Holy Spirit within and among His people. Yes, there is a sense

> **Real worship is not just something we do in a church building. It is the lifestyle and passion of a true Christian 24/7.**

that when we come together we are enjoying a unique experience of worship in community. But maybe it would be better for us to pray, "Thank You Lord that Your presence has come into us."

I was recently at a prayer service with hundreds in attendance as the worship leaders prompted us to sing a line repeatedly: "Fill this temple." The set-up of the song clearly led the crowd to focus on the building as the "temple." It would have been most helpful had someone clarified a new covenant understanding of what this line might mean. The temple is my heart. The temple is the gathered church. Jesus did not die to sanctify a building or an atmosphere. He shed His blood to redeem, transform, fill, and empower human lives by His indwelling Spirit. The tragedy is that we sometimes fail to emphasize and teach boldly about the glorious reality of the indwelling presence of Christ *in* us. Colin Krause offers a balanced view of how we might think of "holy places":

This should caution us about thinking the worship of God is tied to sacred places today, whether that be in church buildings, holy cities (Jerusalem, Rome or Canterbury) or holy sites (the Church of the Nativity, the Church of the Holy Sepulcher *etc.*). It is good to visit these places to gain historic perspective and increase our sense of the reality of what we believe, but to think that one's worship of God is more acceptable in such places, or that we are somehow closer to God in these places, is to deny the truth of Jesus' teaching.[9]

FORM VS. REALITY

In my years of pastoral ministry, I have often tried to clarify for people the difference between "form" and "reality." In stepping into traditional, established churches, I interacted with hundreds of people who miss these spiritual realities of New Testament worship only to become fixated on and defensive of their preferred forms. It could be styles of music, the arrangement of the platform, the use of certain instruments, the level of the lighting, their inclination for certain designs of acceptable clothing, and even the personality and style of a preacher. The more we understand the reality of true worship the less we will be attached to and reliant upon superficial forms.

This is why it is so important to teach on the inside-out work of the Holy Spirit through the gospel. Outside-in thinking anchors us to external aspects of our worship that can distract and even irritate us. Inside-out thinking helps us to transcend the "forms" that might not be to our liking because our emphasis is on what God is doing in me, not on the superficial elements that might be happening around me.

In my midthirties I was called as pastor to a church immediately following the legacy of a forty-year predecessor. He was much more conservative about certain forms than I was and his traditions were deeply entrenched. After my arrival, old and young alike began to attend our prayer summits and experience a fresh work of the indwelling Spirit in various environments. Soon their firm adherence to preferred forms began to loosen. A

> **Inside-out thinking helps us to transcend the "forms" that might not be to our liking because our emphasis is on what God is doing in me, not on the superficial elements that might be happening around me.**

few years later, after spending a weekend at our church, a visiting pastor from New York commented to me, "You have the youngest old people I have ever seen." I was overjoyed by his observation. When spiritual reality captivates our hearts, our concern over superficial forms no longer sours our attitudes.

BUILDINGS AS A KINGDOM TOOL

I have led congregations that have invested scores of millions in property and buildings. Yes, the facilities were very helpful tools allowing families to be served in safe and comfortable environments. Our facilities provided a functional venue for Christians to gather for worship and teaching. Community concerts, mission-focused conferences, feeding programs—and much more—occurred on and beyond our campus. Yet the reality of ministry was not the brick and mortar. The reality of these efforts was the people, inhabited by the Holy Spirit, doing an eternal work through the various means of gospel service and outreach.

Over the years our family has lived in several houses that we truly loved. We made precious memories in these residential structures. But these houses were "homes" because of what we experienced and who we experienced it with. Tragic as it might be, a house could burn down. The loss would be heartbreaking. But the reality of family continues as the supreme value.

Jesus stated that "where [our] treasure is, there [our] heart will be also" (Matt. 6:21). Because of the economic investment in church buildings, the heart and attention of people can become focused on real estate, facilities, and the physical tools that we use to try to enhance our worship.

I've been privileged to travel to over forty-five countries in my decades of ministry, worshiping with believers in most of those locations. Whether an elaborate old structure in Eastern Europe, a secretive cinderblock room in mainland China, or a dirt field in central Africa, the reality of the worship transcended any physical trappings.

Worship is not about pipe organs, hymnals, mega sound systems, digital lights, or atmospheric smoke. Because of Jesus' death, burial, and resurrection, those who worship God do so in spirit and in truth. Real worship transcends our buildings, technology, and music styles. Jesus is the focus and fulfillment of our worship.

Sadly, our emphasis away from the inside-out work of the Holy Spirit has resulted in a widespread redefinition of the word *church*. Generally, people think of "church" as a building. When someone says "I go to First Church," the reference is commonly to a facility on the corner of Fifth and Main, not the people. Yet the Greek word *ekklesia* literally means a "called out assembly." The New Testament emphasis is on people, called by the gospel, who gather and minister in His name. This is what Jesus meant when He said, "I will build my church" (Matt. 16:18). This is the meaning in all of the references to "church" in the New Testament. Nowhere in Scripture do we find that the church is dependent or even clearly attached to buildings.

JESUS AS THE TEMPLE

In the Old Testament, God made it clear that He would not be restricted to temples made by man (1 Kings 8:27; 2 Chron. 2:6; Isa. 66:1). The early church came to understand in a very practical way that connection with God was through Christ, not physical structures (they didn't even have buildings until the fourth century). Christ was the fulfillment of the Old Testament foreshadowing of God's plan.

Jesus had announced, "I tell you, something greater than the temple is here" (Matt. 12:6). John 1:14 explains, "And the Word became flesh and dwelt among us, and we have seen his glory, glory as of the only Son from the Father, full of grace and truth." God's truth and the worship of God was fulfilled in Jesus. "True worship for John [was] worship in terms of Jesus—inspired by the Spirit of Jesus and according to the truth revealed in Jesus."[10]

Jesus' clarification to the woman at the well that He was indeed the Messiah (John 4:25–26) may not have been entirely clear to her, but it was to Him. Jesus, as the One sent from heaven to atone for the sin of mankind, would become the new temple— superseding any structures or locations previously embraced. John Piper summarizes the takeaway concerning Jesus' intention in this conversation: "I am the new temple. When I raise my body from the dead, everywhere in all the world, people may come to

God through me. There will be no pilgrimage to Jerusalem. . . . There will only [be] movement of the heart."[11]

MAN-MADE TEMPLES
VS. JESUS THE TEMPLE

In his sermon, just prior to martyrdom, Stephen exposed the superficial religion and disobedience of the Jews. He described Israel's tent in the wilderness and then the temple Solomon built. He then declared:

> "Yet the Most High does not dwell in houses made by hands, as the prophet says, 'Heaven is my throne, and the earth is my footstool. What kind of house will you build for me, says the Lord, or what is the place of my rest? Did not my hand make all these things?'" (Acts 7:48–50)

Stephen irritated these leaders by questioning their focus on worship that was attached to a physical structure. He went on to reprove these Jewish leaders for being stiff-necked and resisting the Holy Spirit, just as their forefathers had done. He closed his prosecutorial sermon by accusing them of betraying and murdering the Righteous One—Jesus the Christ, the object of true worship (Acts 7:51–53).

Paul, in presenting the truth of Christ and His resurrection at Mars Hill, declared to the Greeks, "The God who made the world and everything in it, being Lord of heaven and earth, does not live in temples made by man" (Acts 17:24). This seemed to be a crucial clarification if people were really going to believe and worship in accordance with the gospel. D. A. Carson clarifies this well:

Under the terms of the old covenant, the temple was the great meeting place between a holy God and his sinful people. This was the place of sacrifice, the place of atonement for sin. But this side of the cross, where Jesus by his sacrifice pays for our sin, Jesus himself becomes the great meeting place between a holy God and his sinful people; thus he becomes the temple, the meeting place between God and his people. It is not as if Jesus in his incarnation adequately serves as the temple of God. That is a huge mistake. Jesus says, "Destroy this temple, and in three days I will raise it up." It is in Jesus' death, in his destruction, and in his resurrection three days later, that Jesus meets our needs and reconciles us to God, becoming the temple, the supreme meeting place between God and sinners. To use Paul's language, we do not simply preach Christ; rather, we preach Christ crucified.[12]

As new covenant believers we must renovate our thinking about the church. First, we must embrace Jesus as the place where God meets man, where the sacrifice has been fulfilled, where intimate worship occurs. We must ask for discernment and faith to see beyond any "forms" or places of worship, and move past the plethora of modern-day encumbrances that confuse our worship. We must ask the Spirit to help us always to "Turn [our] eyes upon Jesus. Look full in His wonderful face" so that "the things of earth," and the temporal trappings of our worship, might "grow strangely dim in the light of His glory and grace."[13]

We must teach passionately about the truth of the gospel that has cleansed our hearts so that we are now indwelt by God's power. Yes, we must say it over and over and over again with deepest gratitude, conviction, and expectation. The transforming presence of the Holy Spirit changes everything, including our worship, from the inside out.

WE ARE THE TEMPLE OF THE HOLY SPIRIT

Jesus has become our "meeting place," and we have become His "meeting place." Jesus, when speaking of the authority He has given to His gathered people, said, "Where two or three are gathered in my name, there am I among them" (Matt. 18:20). Paul describes us as the "body of Christ" (1 Cor. 12:12–13 NLT). We are the physical representation of His life on earth. This is only true because His Spirit indwells our lives.

Paul used other metaphors to describe the dynamic of God's people as a gospel embodiment of worship. "Do you not know that you are God's temple and that God's Spirit dwells in you? If anyone destroys God's temple, God will destroy him. For God's temple is holy, and you are that temple" (1 Cor. 3:16–17). Here, he warns us to revere his collective temple as holy and not to in any way be destroyed or polluted by sinful destructive behavior. Both Paul and Peter used the metaphor of God's people being like a building with Christ as the Cornerstone, the One who establishes us as His holy temple of worship (1 Cor. 3:9; Eph. 2:20–21; 1 Peter 2:5).

The building is only the "house of the Lord" at any given time when believers are there. The "house of the Lord" can be a band of persecuted followers gathered in a home in Cuba, or an outdoor circle of young people praying under a starlit sky. As David Peterson writes, "The New Testament teaches that God's dwelling on earth is no special building or sanctuary within a building; it is the people of God themselves. We are the temple of the Lord."[14] I've experienced church in both environments.

YOU ARE THE TEMPLE OF THE HOLY SPIRIT

At a more personal level, we also know that each individual Christian is a temple of the Holy Spirit in Christ. As a serious call to avoid all kinds of immorality, Paul told the Corinthian believers, "Or do you not know that your body is a temple of the Holy Spirit within you, whom you have from God? You are not your own, for you were bought with a price. So glorify God in your body" (1 Cor. 6:19–20). As those inhabited by the Holy Spirit, we are vessels in whom worship occurs and through whom the Holy Spirit fulfills His purpose to glorify Christ.

CONCENTRIC TEMPLES

I like the way author and professor Harold Best describes New Testament worship as "Temples within temples within a Temple."[15] I am the temple of the Holy Spirit, living as part of the temple of the church. We are all "in Christ." He is our Temple— the reality and focus of our worship.

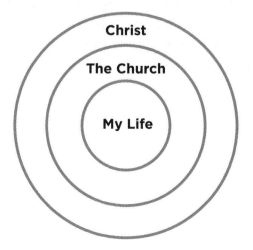

Conversely, from a very personal standpoint, Christ, the Temple, is *in* me. I am indwelt by His Spirit. I am also part of the church—a collective temple. So, functionally, He is the Temple, within my temple, within our temple. As individual believers you and I are the temple of God. We gather with other believers to experience the communal worship of the Christ.

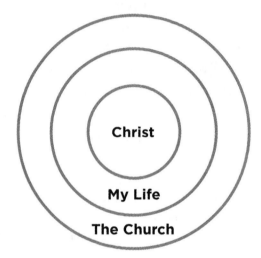

So don't be like Grandma Louise. Resist the urge to go back to something inferior. Jesus, our true Temple, has welcomed us to worship through His gospel. We gather in His name. We are His body, His temple, His building. We are the house of the Lord.

"The heaven above becomes the heaven within; the Savior enthroned at God's right hand becomes the enthroned Lord of our heart and being, and God Himself removes His tabernacle from heaven to earth, and dwells in very deed with men, and in the temple of the believing heart." —A. B. Simpson

"We must desire to know more of God's presence in our lives, and pray for a display of unleashed, reforming, revivifying power among us, dreading all steps that aim to domesticate God. But such prayer and hunger must always be tempered with joyful submission to the constraints of biblical discipline." —D. A. Carson

EXPERIENCE THE GOD WHO ALREADY "SHOWED UP"

The Indwelling Spirit Works In and Through Me to Manifest His Presence

The worship flowed seamlessly on a sunny Lord's Day morning. Easter Sunday was always special. Lyrics celebrating Christ's resurrection drew hundreds of voices into blended choruses of joy.

Unannounced and clearly off script, Pastor Lawrence stepped to the platform, motioning the band to a sudden stop. The interruption was abrupt and baffling to the platform team. The congregation stood perplexed. With consternation paralyzing his own facial expression he gave the strangest of all his announcements in the eleven years of his role as lead pastor.

"The Holy Spirit has left the building!" He seemed sure about his confounding proclamation. Shock waves reverberated throughout the crowd. This was certainly the most perplexing thing they'd ever heard from the platform at the First Evangelical Free Church. Some quietly wondered if the pastor was having a nervous breakdown. Others trusted his prompting but struggled to make sense of his words. How did he know that the presence of God had left the premises? What exactly did that mean? If it was true, what could they do?

I'm guessing you've never heard such an announcement and I doubt you ever will. Why? First, no one would ever want such an "Ichabod" moment during a worship gathering. We need and cherish the work of the Holy Spirit when we gather in Jesus' name. Second, because the Holy Spirit was never really about the "building" to start with (as we saw in the last chapter). Physical temples and buildings are not His primary interest in the new covenant. Third, for the Holy Spirit to truly "leave the building," He would have to vacate the heart of every worshiper.

Bizarre as the story of Pastor Lawrence may seem, it begs a question: If the idea of the Holy Spirit leaving the building does not register with New Testament teaching, why are we so obsessed with the Holy Spirit "coming into" the building? Is there any clear teaching in the New Testament to substantiate that often-repeated idea in our earnest songs and well-intended commentary?[1]

DID GOD "SHOW UP"?

In a real-life moment, I sat recently in a large church in the West, preparing to speak in the Sunday services. The lead pastor, an energetic, godly leader, was sharing some announcements with the congregation. Referring back to the previous weekend's service, he declared, "God really showed up!" Now, I instinctively knew what he was trying to say. In essence, he was grateful the Lord had worked powerfully in the hearts of the people in ways that were evident and Christ-honoring.

But apart from my internal reinterpretation of his comment, I wondered, "Where was God before He decided to 'show up'?" How do you know He "showed up"? How do we biblically judge a "show up" service versus a "no show" gathering? Is there any New Testament verse to verify this description?

In another context in the Southeast, I remember a pastor stating that "the Holy Spirit was thick" in a particular event. Now, I know this is not a reference to body mass. Rather, this is an expression of some sense that the Holy Spirit worked in an unusual way in a particular context. But again, I ask: "What makes the Holy Spirit 'thick' vs. 'thin'?"

In a recent pre-service prayer time at a conference in Canada, a fellow speaker prayed that the Holy Spirit would "hover" above the crowd. At that same conference another prayed that the Holy Spirit would invade the room. Another prayed that the Holy Spirit would "blow on us." Well-meaning and spiritually eager Christians will often "invite" the Holy Spirit to "come" into the gathering." Similarly, it is frequently said that we "welcome" the Holy Spirit. We speak of the Holy Spirit descending on a service. I could go on (and on) accounting for these popular but ambiguous descriptions used in countless contexts, including church services, prayer meetings, mass concerts, or lyrics played on the Christian radio.

Again, these are evocative and apparently sincere gestures, but are they actually biblical? Is it really important that we use New Testament language to describe the work of the Holy Spirit? Do our words really matter all that much?

What do we believe about the nature and work of the Holy Spirit when we speak like this? Is He reluctantly hiding in the rafters waiting for us to compel Him to join us based on some level of faith that we stir up? Is one part of the person of the Holy Spirit "in" us while the rest of Him (the really sensational part) must be summoned to appear in some fashion in our midst? What makes this chapter so difficult is that these kinds of words have been written about and uttered by some great "giants of the faith." This is the language of people I love and respect. I have also used this vocabulary in years past but have become uncomfortable and unconvinced of their biblical veracity. I can't help but wonder, "What are we really saying?" What criteria are we using to evaluate a powerful work of the Holy Spirit? What "stimuli" gives validity to our sense of the Holy Spirit at work? What clear New Testament teaching even supports this kind of language? Could it be that we are confusing countless Christ followers about the person and work of the third person of the Trinity?

I believe we want the same thing. We want the full reality of all Jesus promised to us in the person of the Holy Spirit. However, the Bible is fully sufficient, especially the gospel language of the Word of God, to give us clear and Christ-honoring words to describe the work of the Spirit. Since the Scriptures were written as a holy "biography" or "operator's manual" for the Spirit, I believe He would be honored if our descriptions of His person and work were consistent with what He has told us about Himself. I also believe that if we do not use His own language, we can create false expectations in the hearts of sincere congregants. Ultimately, disappointment settles in as we anchor our spiritual hopes in these old covenant, or even unbiblical, declarations.

HE ALREADY SHOWED UP

"That's not what I said!" "I didn't do that!" "He doesn't really know me!" "That never happened!" These are common expressions of someone who feels they have been misrepresented. Misrepresentation is one of the most frustrating dynamics in the human experience. To be misrepresented by a friend, a critic, a gossip, or a public report is infuriating. Whatever the motive, the effect is troubling. All of us like to be portrayed to others as accurately as possible. We want to be known correctly and honestly.

The popular satirical Christian website, *Babylon Bee*, offered the humorous story of a church where "the power of God as manifested in the third Person of the Trinity patiently waited in the foyer through several songs Sunday morning, before finally entering into the main sanctuary to flood the place and fill the atmosphere as the gathered worshipers broke into" a particular chorus.[2]

Imagine a husband and wife who have enjoyed an evening of intimate and meaningful conversation for several hours, when one of them suddenly blurts out, "I wish you would just talk to me!" Or a parent who faithfully attends every one of her ten-year-old son's little league soccer games (and even practices), and one evening, he cries, "I wish you would just support me in my soccer activities!" Or a group of coworkers sharing a dinner, with Bill, the supervisor, seated at the head of the table, fully engaged in the conversation, but one employee says, "Too bad Bill couldn't be here tonight." These scenarios are confounding, irrational, and demeaning.

For years, even as a pastor, I wanted the "glory to fall" (we will say more about this in chapter 8) and the "manifest presence" to arrive, but I was failing to realize that, in Christ, and in the fullest sense, He has and is showing us His glory.

One of the most treasured titles given to Jesus is "Immanuel" —God with us. Of course He was "with" people during His earthly ministry. "The Word became flesh and dwelt among us, and we have seen his glory, glory as of the only Son from the

Father, full of grace and truth" (John 1:14). He literally taberna-
cled in our midst as the manifestation of the presence of God. The
doctrine of the incarnation reminds us that Jesus took on human
flesh, lived a sinless life, spoke authoritative teaching, willingly
died via crucifixion as our substitute, and lives in glorious resurrection power. He is the mediator of a new covenant. He is now
with us—even more, the glory of Jesus is *in* us (John 14:16; Rom.
8:10; Eph. 3:16, 20; Col. 1:27).

I have not been able to find any teaching in the New Testament that indicates the fullness of His life is outside us and must
be summoned to "show up." He has already promised to be "in our
midst" when we gather (Matt. 18:20 NASB). He did not offer some
condition that we must meet, some formula we must discover, or
some lyric we must sing in order to experience His presence in
and among us. He never said He would reluctantly hang out in
the rafters until we coerce Him to enter the room. The one who
promised, "I will never leave you or forsake you" (Heb. 13:5) has
not drifted away in forgetful-
ness of His finished work or
sure word.

As a reminder, we have
already seen that the Spirit's
purpose is always to glorify
Jesus. We must embrace all
that Christ accomplished
and know that He wants us
to live in the reality of his new
covenant—a covenant that
has provided the indwelling
Spirit. In previous chapters
we have affirmed that the

> **We do not need to summon or invite the Holy Spirit as if there is some "outside-in" effect that we must seek. No, the work of the Spirit is an "inside-out" power and promise that transforms us from glory to glory.**

Holy Spirit is a person, not a "force." We live in the confidence that we *are* the temple of the Lord. Now, it is clear that we do not need to summon or invite the Holy Spirit as if there is some "outside-in" effect that we must seek. No, the work of the Spirit is an "inside-out" power and promise that transforms us from glory to glory. There is no new covenant teaching I can find that compels us to look for the Holy Spirit in the atmosphere. Rather, we are taught repeatedly to live in the fulfilled promise of His presence in our sanctified hearts, in gratitude for the finished work of Christ. Based on what He has written about Himself—He works in the heart, transforming the life, ministering through every believer in supernatural grace, and has already showed up.

I have concluded that much heresy, aberrant Christian practice, and even our mainstream pursuits of some new and novel experience are rooted in a diminished view of the supremacy of the person and work of Christ, and a misguided understanding of the sufficiency of the indwelling Spirit in our lives. My friend Robbie Symons says it this way: "You'll never stare into the face of Jesus Christ and be let down. Jesus is like the sun in our solar system. He is our sufficiency. . . . If He is the sun for our soul, we must catch some rays!"[3]

The glory of God is Jesus *in* us—not floating above us, around us, hovering in the building or waiting in the lobby until we find the right formula to coax Him in. Bob Kauflin writes, "We reference drawing near to God with no mention of Christ or his finished work. It's an unmediated presence, something we can experience without an awareness of what Jesus did to make it possible. That kind of understanding leads us to start looking for the right combination, the right password, the right 'secret' to experience God's presence again."[4]

RETHINKING MANIFEST PRESENCE

Because of my love for prayer and my yearning for a true revival of the church, I have often borrowed a traditional term. We call it "manifest presence." The term is not in the New Testament. In my circles, we tend to speak of it as a common new covenant phrase, even though it isn't. Yet we sincerely long for a powerful, evident work of the Holy Spirit. Admittedly, I have struggled to find the right words to describe what we long for and have even experienced in the past.

Believe me, I love the hope of what we call "manifest presence" as much as anyone. I've seen the Holy Spirit working in profound, extraordinary ways countless times. Whether it was a movement of palpable surrender in a Sunday gathering, an unprecedented response to the Word at the end of a service, or a profound brokenness in a prayer meeting. What I have seen and sensed is very real. In scores of prayer summits, I've seen proud people broken, confessing lifelong habitual sin and being delivered through the prayers of believing friends. I've witnessed profound moments of renewal in gatherings in nations across the world.

The question is not whether the Holy Spirit works in overwhelming ways at times—He does. The question is *how* does this happen and *why*? Our answer must be a clear *gospel* answer—not one taken exclusively from old covenant incidences, dramatic stories from the past, or traditional phrases we've perpetuated. We must use biblical language to describe a biblical work. This will clear the confusion, align our expectations, and set us on a course for something very powerful according to the New Testament plan of God for our lives and churches.

NEW COVENANT MANIFESTATION

In the original language, the word "manifest" means "to make apparent, present or evident to the experiences or senses." In the New Testament, it primarily refers to the manifestation of the character and plan of God in the person and work of Jesus (Mark 4:22; John 17:6; Rom. 3:21; 1 Tim. 3:16; 1 John 1:2). Romans 10:12 speaks of Jesus "bestowing [manifesting] his riches on all who call on him," whether Jew or Greek. Similarly, Romans 10:20 speaks of God manifesting Himself through the gospel to the Gentiles.

First John 3:10 teaches that the manifestation of genuine faith to the world is rooted in our righteous lives and love for one another. Similarly, 2 Corinthians 4:2 (KJV) speaks of the manifestation of the truth, through the work of God's Word in our lives, to the consciences of the lost. It seems the actual teaching about "manifestation" is very different than our current language about "manifest presence."

> **The manifestation of genuine faith to the world is rooted in our righteous lives and love for one another.**

In John 14:21, Jesus said, "he who loves me will be loved by my Father, and I will love him and manifest myself to him." He made this statement in the context of teaching His disciples in the upper room concerning the Holy Spirit. By way of the indwelling Spirit, Jesus said He would manifest Himself to them. A common New Testament explanation I have often used for what I have called "manifest presence" is found in 1 Corinthians 14:24–25: "But if all prophesy, and an unbeliever or outsider enters, he is convicted by all, he is called to account by all, the secrets of his heart are disclosed, and so, falling on his face, he will worship God and declare that God is really among you."

Paul brings clarity and order to the use of gifts in the Corinthian gatherings, warning them about the danger of practices that would, no doubt, confuse unbelievers who enter in. These verses make it clear that when prophecy, the declaration of gospel truth, is central, unbelievers are undeniably affected by the reality of the living Christ in the midst of His people. It becomes clear that Christians are not practicing religion but are in a relationship with the risen and indwelling Lord, who is working in their midst.

But this text does not indicate that God is among us in a way that He was not previously. Rather, it explains how an unbeliever comes to recognize our consistent experience of the indwelling presence of the Holy Spirit. In this context, the sense of God's presence is rooted in the powerful proclamation and display of the truth, through the lives of Spirit-indwelt believers, thus affecting the conscience of unregenerate people.

I wrote in my book *Transforming Prayer* that the glory of God is "the magnification of the person of Christ on the lips of his people and the manifestation of the presence of Christ *in* the lives of His people."[5] I believe we can affirm clear New Testament teaching that underscores this.

NEW TESTAMENT "MANIFEST PRESENCE"

Earlier in Paul's instructions about the proper understanding of Christian gatherings (chapters 12–14), he spoke directly and clearly of a "manifestation of the Spirit" (1 Cor. 12:7; see also 14:12). I have come to believe that what we typically describe as the "manifest presence" of God is more biblically explained as "the manifestation of the Spirit" (words clearly in the New Testament). This occurs through the work of the Spirit *in* and then *through* the individual believers as they are gathered in worship and ministry. Here's what Paul says:

> Now there are varieties of gifts, but the same Spirit; and there are varieties of service, but the same Lord; and there are varieties of activities, but it is the same God who empowers them all in *everyone*. To *each* is given the *manifestation of the Spirit* for the common good. For to one is given through the Spirit the utterance of wisdom, and to another the utterance of knowledge according to the same Spirit, to another faith by the same Spirit, to another gifts of healing by the one Spirit, to another the working of miracles, to another prophecy, to another the ability to distinguish between spirits, to another various kinds of tongues, to another the interpretation of tongues. All these are empowered by one and *the same Spirit*, who apportions to each one individually as he wills. (1 Cor. 12:4–11)

Again, in this book I am not interested in engaging in debates about the specific gifts and their use. Regardless of what you believe about certain gifts, one thing is clear here. Manifest presence is not the mystery we have made of it. It is about a commitment to mutual ministry where many parts of the body contribute to the glory of Christ by allowing the Spirit to use them in building up one another. This is new covenant manifest presence.[6]

Thankfully, many churches seek to facilitate this kind of experience in small groups, ministry teams, and other interactive gatherings. We should definitely celebrate this. But in our congregational gatherings (which is the context of 1 Corinthians 12–14),

> Manifest presence is not the mystery we have made of it. It is about a commitment to mutual ministry where many parts of the body contribute to the glory of Christ by allowing the Spirit to use them in building up one another.

believers seldom have opportunity to minister to one another, greatly restricting the manifesting of the presence of the Holy Spirit in and through their lives in essential ministry for Christ and to one another. Instead of this expressly New Testament experience, we tend to emphasize platforms, personalities, performances, presentations, and programs. The original design for the "assembly" has morphed into an event-oriented focus where we can feel pressured to program some semblance of the Holy Spirit at work.

We long for a deep, transforming sense of the Holy Spirit and the Word when we gather. But somewhere along the way it seems we have downplayed the avenues where the Spirit works freely, even spontaneously, through the gifted and gathered believers. As a result, the assembly can become a passive "crowd" rather than a functioning body. As Carl Hoch has noted, "A church that loses community becomes merely an organization whose members feel like cogs in a huge machine that grinds along regardless of their needs," turning people into "faceless non-entities."[7]

As author David Peterson reminds us that the description of public worship in 1 Corinthians 12–14 "speaks to us of the value and importance of spontaneous, verbal ministries of exhortation, comfort or admonition by congregational members (cf. 1 Thes. 4:18; 5:11, 14; Eph. 4:15). Such mutual ministry is often confined to the home group, or to times of personal interaction after church services. Why is it not also encouraged in the public gathering of the whole church? . . . There should be some space for the informal contributions of members."[8] He affirms that the Lord works powerfully as believers gather in His name "through the ministry which he enables them to have to one another, as an outworking of the promises of the new covenant. We meet with God when we meet with one another."[9]

THE MAIN EVENT?

Today, it seems the main event at church is to attend primarily in the interest of hearing a preacher, a component that typically comprises more the 50 percent of the gathering. Acts 2:42 explains that the early church continued steadfastly in the "apostle's teaching and the fellowship, to the breaking of bread and the prayers." Preaching was definitely an essential component. It is important that biblically astute leaders guard the doctrine and guide the order of the church. I am a passionate preacher—so I like that part. But according to this formula, we might say this was more like one-fourth of the equation. Norman Grubb discusses the priority of mutual exhortation in describing the work of revival. He notes:

> The early church was first and foremost a fellowship. . . .
> When they met in worship. . . . It was a living fellowship in action. All took part. . . . We have now replaced fellowshipping by preaching in our modern life, and the reason is not hard to find. Fellowshipping necessitates a real flow of life in the fellowship, for each person has to be ready to contribute his share of what the Lord is really saying to him: Preaching is an easy way for a not-too-living fellowship. . . .

In the Scriptures it is also obvious that an important part of fellowshipping was to be mutual exhortation, not just public exhortation by a preacher but each one exhorting the other.[10]

The New Testament gives many instructions about the priority of mutual ministry. The apostle Peter, through whom the Spirit worked so powerfully in the early church, offers clear instruction for the glory of God in the church:

> As *each* has received a gift, use it to serve one another, as good stewards of God's varied grace: whoever speaks, as one who speaks oracles of God; whoever serves, as one who serves by the strength that God supplies—in order that in everything God may be glorified through Jesus Christ. To him belong glory and dominion forever and ever. Amen. (1 Peter 4:10–11)

In Romans 12:1–8, Paul likewise calls the church to sacrificial surrender (as worship) and the faithful use of their gifts in building up one another. Hebrews 3:13 tells us to exhort one another so that we are not "hardened by the deceitfulness of sin." Similarly, Hebrews 10:24–25 commands that we not forsake our assembling together. James 5:16 calls us to mutual confession of sin and prayer for one another.

It is clear to me that in New Testament times, the leadership of the Holy Spirit was much more dynamic in and through the body than it is today. The sacrosanct forms we have created, which now focus on the gifts of only a few key people, should be reevaluated in the interest of New Testament teaching. Perhaps the manifest presence of God is much more clear and practical than we think.

IF I HAD TO DO IT OVER

The biggest regret of my entire pastoral ministry is that I never took the reality of what we experienced in prayer summits into the mainstream of our weekend gatherings. Tradition dies hard. Control is tantamount. As Jim Cymbala says, "the microphone can be a drug." Predictability is our security. It may be that the spectator and consumer-oriented culture of our society has tethered us too closely to carefully scripted services. I believe we need a serious reevaluation of what we are really doing on weekends in this thing we call "church." None of us wants to relegate our worship to some superficial replacement of what Paul taught as the norm for the experience of Christ among His gathered people. The manifest presence of the Holy Spirit is truly available to new covenant believers. The instruction book has not changed.

FROM ONE HEART TO ANOTHER

Personally, I have concluded that I need to stop petitioning the Lord for His "manifest presence" and start practicing what He has already instructed about this important reality. Rather than being compelled to *see* the manifest presence of God, we should be committed to *be* the manifest presence of God.

One of the real tests of a pastor's belief in the power and sufficiency of the Holy Spirit is a commitment to free the people up to do more ministry, based on their gifts, even in the general assembly of our Lord's Day gatherings. To seek the manifest presence of the Spirit but to neglect the clear guidelines of the New Testament is to pray one way and to act another. I know this is radical and requires a reassessment of our church models.[11] We may not need to totally renovate, but at least should intentionally integrate.

> **Rather than being compelled to *see* the manifest presence of God, we should be committed to *be* the manifest presence of God.**

Over the years, I've seen and heard about stories of "mercy drops" of revival that started when the Word of God was received in humility and some honest and desperate soul came to a place of personal and then public surrender—confessing sin, desiring radical obedience, passionate for reconciliation. The pastor gave up the power of the microphone. In going public, surrendered souls sparked a similar response in the hearts of others. They, too, came to a place of conviction from the Word of God. The Spirit of God took control of their yielded hearts and movements of heartfelt obedience, exhortation, and earnest intercession for one another—all sparked something holy and special. The work of the Spirit became evident in the church.

The core catalyst to this work is surrender. The Holy Spirit takes control of and works through one heart, then two, ten, hundreds, thousands. Norman Grubb describes it as a work that "leaps from one heart to another."[12] The Spirit does this, not to produce some human-centered effect, but to glorify Jesus and advance the work of the gospel.

This is the new covenant cause and catalyst of what we call "manifest presence." Members exhibit an earnest response to the gospel truth of Jesus Christ preached and applied. They are free to engage in mutual ministry and exhortation toward one another. Participants surrender in bold faith to a sure promise and transforming, inside-out work of the Spirit, desiring to be used to build up others—not chasing an outside-in experience, but rather, cherishing and committing to an inside-out work of the Holy Spirit.

I remember an afternoon at a prayer summit when the men were gathering in various locations, 15–20 per group. The Word of Christ was indeed dwelling in us richly as we had been reading passages of Scripture to one another and singing in spontaneous praise throughout the day. The conviction of the Holy Spirit was evident as the Word began to work deeply to expose sin and stir deep repentance. One by one, men began to seek the prayers of the other men in the room. This was another genuine, unforced, Spirit-prompted application of James 5:16: "Therefore, confess your sins to one another and pray for one another, that you may be healed. The prayer of a righteous person has great power as it is working."

These moments were so powerful that we prayed right through the dinner hour as men "[wept] with those who [wept]" (Rom. 12:15) and prayed from the Scriptures in powerful intercession and admonition for one another. We moved immediately into the evening large-group celebration of the Lord's Table. Food seemed secondary. God's presence was "manifest" as the internal work of the Spirit leapt "from one heart to another." Having seen this happen time after time gives me a longing for more of this reality in the church.

THE MANIFESTATION OF
THE SPIRIT = THE GLORY OF CHRIST

To speak, in any fashion, of the Holy Spirit as a "force" in the environment is at best a distraction away from the completed work of Christ that secured our cleansed and holy hearts, where we now experience and express the presence of a person—the very

Spirit of Christ. Rather than praying for the arrival of a "manifest presence," we would do better to facilitate the New Testament approach for the promised "manifestation of the Spirit." This testifies of the power of the gospel and the transforming work of Christ in us, convicting the conscience of unbelievers and compelling them to give full consideration, not to some mysterious collective experience, but to the good news of the gospel. This is how the Holy Spirit makes the new covenant work of Jesus apparent, present, or evident to the experiences or senses of people.

NEW COVENANT CLARITY REQUIRED

At this point, it's possible that your experiences, assumptions, or traditions are making you skeptical. But regardless of our past or long-held beliefs, we have to ask ourselves: What does the Bible actually teach? We cannot promote and pursue old covenant ideas and expect a real new covenant work. Further, we cannot promote things that are not taught. To do so is to diminish the full implications of the gospel.

Recently, in a book about the Holy Spirit, I read these perplexing opening words: "There was something different about the atmosphere that surrounded the apostle Peter."[13] The rest of the book is somewhat of an apologetic for atmospheric experiences that manifest the Holy Spirit, most very hard to validate from New Testament teaching. The author encourages the reader to "host" more of the "presence."

To reiterate, Jesus did not die to sanctify an atmosphere. He shed His blood to sanctify—and fill—hearts. There was nothing special about the atmosphere around Peter. The Holy Spirit is not like the dust cloud that hovered around Charlie Brown's friend,

Pig Pen. He does not work in the ambiance of the building or some "aura" afloat around us

There was something very powerful about the Spirit that *indwelt* Peter, gifted him, led him, and ministered through him. Here is the good news. Empowering news. That same Spirit lives in you. He has called and gifted you. He wants to use you. Paul taught that, "we have this treasure in earthen vessels, that the excellence of the power may be of God and not of us" (2 Cor. 4:7 NKJV). This is the truth of the new covenant. The indwelling Holy Spirit wants to manifest the excellent power of His life through you.

"It is of the highest importance from the standpoint of worship that we decide whether the Holy Spirit is a Divine Person, worthy to receive our adoration, our faith, our love, and our entire surrender to Himself, or whether it is simply an influence emanating from God or a power or an illumination that God imparts to us. If the Holy Spirit is a person, and a Divine Person, and we do not know Him as such, then we are robbing a Divine Being of the worship and faith and the love and the surrender to Himself which are His due." —R. A. TORREY

"A person who is drunk, we say, is 'under the influence' of alcohol; and certainly a Spirit-filled Christian is under the influence and power of the Holy Spirit. . . . Under the influence of the Holy Spirit we do not lose control; we gain it."
—JOHN R. STOTT

SEEK A "FILLING," NOT A "FALLING"

The Indwelling Spirit Controls Me in Order to Change My Attitudes and Relationships

The old familiar chorus of the song "Spirit of the Living God" expresses a sincere prayer that the Spirit would "fall afresh on me."[1] A newer remake of this classic chorus even includes a phrase calling on the Holy Spirit to come "in the room."[2]

One popular song invites the Spirit to flood the facility with an appeal for His glory to "fall." The song was inspired by a dream by one of the musical artists.[3] She dreamt one night of standing in an old church building where rain was falling from the ceiling and flooding the floor—thus leading to some creative lyrics that have inspired many young worshipers. The lyrics may be catchy and the songwriters popular, but does this really represent new covenant truth?

More and more songs are being downloaded to the local worship team's "Planning Center" that speak in artistic and rhythmic form of God opening the heavens, coming down, filling the building, etc. So, as believers living in the new covenant, how do we sort

through this? In a New Testament sense, how do you explain this?
Instead of singing for the Spirit to "fall afresh on" us, we should
pray that He would *work* afresh *within* us. As we've already seen,
the clear implication of the gospel and New Testament teaching is
centered on the profound truth of the indwelling Holy Spirit, not
a hopeful or potential arrival of a divine presence.

Over the centuries and today, songwriters from all kinds of
backgrounds have undoubtedly been earnest, longing for the
full work of the Holy Spirit. But words matter. Do our worship
songs reflect the true teaching of the new covenant which we now
embrace because of the sufficient and complete work of Christ?
What difference does it make today?

THE "FALLING" SPIRIT

The description of the Spirit falling on people is definitely in the
Bible. In the Old Testament, the Spirit "came upon" (KJV) various individuals to empower them for their God-assigned tasks.
We see this to be true of judges (Judg. 3:10; 6:34; 11:29; 13:25;
14:19; 15:14), craftsmen (Ex. 31:3–6; 1 Chron. 28:11–12),
prophets (1 Chron. 12:18; 2 Chron. 15:1–7; 20:14–17; 24:20;
Num. 24:2), and civil administrators like Moses and his seventy
assistants (Num. 11:17), Joshua (Num. 27:19), Saul (1 Sam.
11:6), and David (1 Sam. 16:13). In some cases, the Spirit only
temporarily resided in them. For example, when God rejected
Saul as king and chose David to replace him, the divine Spirit left
Saul and came upon David (1 Sam. 16:13–14).[4] Other prophets, especially those who wrote the Scriptures, seemed to be
continuously empowered by the Spirit both for their reception
of God's Word and their authoritative proclamation of it.[5] (At
transformingpresencebook.com, I have explained in more detail

the work of the Holy Spirit in the Old Testament.)

How does the Holy Spirit relate to non-Christians? Put simply, He works upon them before He works within them. He works upon them to convict of sin, righteousness, and judgment. Jesus said this would be His function in the world John 16:8–11.[6]

On the day of Pentecost, the new covenant promise of God's transforming presence was realized as the assembled believers were filled with the Holy Spirit and the church was birthed for the supernatural spread of the gospel into all the world (Acts 1:8). Peter connected this event to the prophecy of Joel (Acts 2:16–21, 33; cf. Joel 2:28–32) where it was predicted that the Spirit would be "pour[ed] out," not just on religious officials or spiritual leaders, but on young and old, male and female alike. By associating this broad filling of the Holy Spirit to the Old Testament perspective of the Jerusalem crowd, Peter was clearly pointing to this amazing initiation of a new day (Acts 2:33, 38). We know it as the church—living in the power of the indwelling Holy Spirit as participants in the new covenant. The New Testament doesn't encourage us to think of a continual "pouring out," but rather a personal "living out" of the indwelling Spirit of God, residing in us through the work of Christ.[7]

> **The New Testament doesn't encourage us to think of a continual "pouring out," but rather a personal "living out" of the indwelling Spirit of God, residing in us through the work of Christ.**

Nowhere in the New Testament do we find a teaching that we are to seek, pray for, or sing about the need for the Spirit to "fall." This is old "outside-in" language rather than the "inside-out" teaching of the new covenant. Yes, the Holy Spirit did fall on several occasions in the book of Acts as the gospel was preached, and the church was established in other locations through the proclamation of the new covenant.[8] But most New Testament scholars would affirm that these instances are "descriptive" of the work of the Spirit, but not "prescriptive." In other words, they tell the story of what happened in the unique unfolding of the Acts narrative, but the accounts do not teach these instances as normal practice for the Christian life. It is safe to say that, from Acts to Revelation, the new covenant teaching is that the Holy Spirit now desires to "fill" the believer.[9] We are clearly commanded to be filled with the Holy Spirit (Eph. 5:18). (For more clarification on how we can rightly understand the events of the book of Acts, see Appendix 1.)

Some traditions have spoken often of the "fullness" of the Holy Spirit, although that specific term does not appear in the New Testament.[10] The use of the term typically points to sanctification, brokenness, full surrender, or even a level of spiritual perfection.

TWO OUTCOMES OF FILLING

The New Testament is clear about the idea of what it means "to be filled" (*pimplesthai*). This Greek word is primarily used by Luke in his gospel and the book of Acts. Another essential New Testament word "to fill" (*pleroun*) is a clear command for Christian living.

These terms are used in two primary ways. First, "to be filled" points to the "sudden inspiration of a moment,"[11] leading to various expressions of supernatural ministry impact. The second usage refers to a person's "governing characteristic, his controlling disposition."[12] As we will see, this refers to the Holy Spirit ruling the heart, mind, and actions of a Christ follower in a consistent way so as to produce the fruit of Christ's character and affect our relationships with others. For both of these results, you and I desperately need the power of the indwelling Spirit.

Filled for Gospel Impact

Various verses in the New Testament speak of a filling of the Holy Spirit that enabled the recipients to minister in supernatural grace. Luke 1:15 speaks of John the Baptist being filled, even from his mother's womb, to be the forerunner of Jesus. In Luke 1:41, John's mother Elizabeth was filled with the Spirit to recognize the divinity of the baby in her cousin Mary's womb. In Luke 1:67, John's father Zacharias was filled with the Holy Spirit so that he would prophesy about Jesus the Messiah. Luke 4:1 references Jesus being full of the Holy Spirit in preparation for His extended time in the wilderness, His temptation by Satan, and His subsequent ministry.

The early disciples were filled with the Spirit on the day of Pentecost (Acts 2:4) and enabled to speak the glories of God in languages they did not humanly know, leading to a great gospel conversion of thousands in conjunction with Peter's sermon. In Acts 4:8, Peter was filled with the Holy Spirit in order to preach the gospel, leading to countless conversions. Later in that chapter, all the believers were "filled with the Holy Spirit and began to speak the word of God with boldness" (4:31).

As the church grew and needed others to administer the beleaguered widow-feeding program, they found seven men "full of the Spirit" to effectively manage this vital task (Acts 6:3). The result was that "the word of God continued to increase, and the number of the disciples multiplied greatly in Jerusalem, and a great many of the priests became obedient to the faith" (6:7).

Among those seven was Stephen, who was notably filled with the Spirit (6:5), not just to serve in the immediate moment but to later preach with power. He also experienced supernatural grace to gloriously magnify Christ as the first Christian martyr (7:55).

After his conversion, Paul was filled with the Holy Spirit (9:17) in preparation for his ministry as the apostle to the Gentiles. Acts 11:24 speaks of Barnabas, who was full of the Holy Spirit and was used to bring many to the Lord and disciple them in the ways of the gospel. As Paul and Barnabas ministered together, Paul was filled again by the Holy Spirit (13:9) to confront an enemy of the gospel who was miraculously blinded by God at Paul's word, with the result that a notable community leader believed the gospel.

Did you notice the common denominator in all of these instances? These "fillings" all resulted in the powerful advancement of the gospel. As Jesus clarified about the Spirit, "He will glorify me" (John 16:14). The Spirit fills His disciples so that they can fulfill the gospel mandate to proclaim truth and make disciples of Jesus Christ.

Filled for Gospel Character

The other result of the filling of the Holy Spirit, primarily taught in New Testament, leads to a progressive lifestyle of Christlikeness. A. B. Simpson says, "The power which the Holy Spirit brings to us is first of all power to be, and then power to do and suffer."[13] One such reference in Acts describes the disciples as being "filled with joy and with the Holy Spirit" (13:52) even in the face of persecution.

The evidence of the controlling influence of the indwelling Spirit of Christ is something we all desire. As we "walk by the Spirit," living moment-by-moment in His power, we live in victory over the destructive desires of the flesh (Gal. 5:16). The fruit (or evident supernatural character) of the Holy Spirit is seen in our lives as we exhibit, "love, joy, peace, patience, kindness, goodness, faithfulness, gentleness, self-control" (Gal. 5:22–23).

THE COMMAND: BE FILLED!

The New Testament never commands the believer to be indwelt, gifted, baptized, sealed, or anointed by the Holy Spirit. All of these are assumed for every believer (Rom. 8:9; 1 Cor. 12:7, 13; Eph. 1:13; 1 John 2:20). These are part of the basic operating system. But we are clearly commanded to be filled with the Holy Spirit. This is essential for our optimal spiritual fruitfulness. Ephesians 5:18 says, "And do not get drunk with wine, for that is debauchery, but be filled with the Spirit."

The distinction is powerful. Gordon Fee explains, "Here the contrast is between being drunken with wine and being filled by the Spirit, with the two imperatives indicating 'never do so' in the former case, and 'always be so' in the latter."[14] To live "under the influence" of alcohol is the epitome of foolishness, lack of self-control, recklessness, and wasteful living. By calling out the danger of this lifestyle, common in his day and in ours, Paul sets up a riveting contrast: "But be filled with the Spirit." This indicates a life controlled by the Holy Spirit, in dissimilarity to a life dominated by drunkenness. D. Martin Lloyd-Jones says, "Being filled with the Spirit is meant to be a constant permanent condition which does not vary and which does not change."[15]

The Greek construction here is important. In summary, this command is in the *imperative mood*, which means this is not optional for the Christ follower. This is a clear directive for our lives.

Also, it is in the *passive voice*, which means that we do not make this happen or drum it up in any way. Rather, this filling happens to us as we yield to the work of the indwelling Spirit. Third, it is in the *present tense*, which makes this a continuous necessity, not a one-time event. As is often noted, the sense is "be *being* filled." Finally, the command is *plural*, which means the command is for every believer. But even more relevant to our corporate worship, it is something we are all to pursue together in our gatherings. A filling, not a falling. D. Martyn Lloyd-Jones gives helpful clarification to a common misunderstanding to this idea of being "filled":

> There is great confusion about all this, and people are waiting for an experience of being filled because they have a wrong conception of this particular teaching. . . . The Holy Spirit is not just an influence. So many seem to talk about being filled with the Spirit as if the Holy Spirit were some kind of liquid. They talk about having an "empty vessel," an empty jug, and having the Spirit poured in. That is entirely wrong because it forgets that the Holy Spirit is a Person. He is not a substance, not a liquid, and not a power like electricity. We all tend to fall into this error. We even tend to refer to the Holy Spirit as "it," forgetting the Holy Spirit is the third Person in the blessed Holy Trinity. Our ideas about being "filled with the Spirit" go entirely wrong just because we have forgotten that He is a Person.[16]

Another teacher elaborates:

> The Holy Spirit is indwelling us already. It is not that some part of the Spirit comes into us and then another part and then another part until we are filled up; this is not the idea.

He is already indwelling us. To be filled means to be taken over completely by His control and power, and means the exclusion of anything that is preventing that power from operating in our lives.

To be filled with the Spirit means to exclude everything that hinders the Spirit's power. It is not to be 90% of the Spirit's will and 10% my own will. For every Christian there is to be a one hundred percent acceptance of the will of the Lord. There is to be no reserve, no reluctance, no dark patches, the whole life is to be given over to the will of the Lord, and when that is so, the Holy Spirit is free to operate in us and promote in us the things that are precious and abiding.[17]

So, as we walk in the Spirit and worship together, we are not looking for some mysterious "falling" from heaven. Rather, we are pursuing full submission to the One who, because of the work of the cross, already indwells us

> **The Holy Spirit motivates our behavior; our behavior does not manufacture the Holy Spirit.**

and longs to transform us from the inside out. Instead of anticipating what the Spirit might do *to* us, we would do well to focus on what Spirit is wanting to do *in* us. As is often said, "The question is not how much of the Holy Spirit do you have, but how much of you does the Holy Spirit have." The Holy Spirit motivates our behavior; our behavior does not manufacture the Holy Spirit.[18]

Klyne Snodgrass writes, "The Spirit is the one who conveys the presence of Jesus to us. Faith creates such a consciousness of the presence of God and Christ *in* us that we have heightened attention about God's desires and a sense of God's work *in* us to enable his will."[19] Author Jeff Kennedy adds a vital application explaining that this is "an actual experience of the Spirit that leads to a greater awareness of Him in our lives."[20] He illustrates this with the example of buying a new car. Prior to the purchase, we seldom notice the model that we now own. Once it is ours, it seems we see similar cars everywhere. He confirms that the greater our actual experience of the Spirit, the greater our awareness of His presence within us. I would add that a true understanding of the filling of the Spirit releases us from a pursuit of a confusing old covenant idea of a "presence" falling form the sky. Rather, we have a dynamic inside-out awareness, confidence, expectation, transformation as promised by Jesus.

WE ARE FILLED!

So what will this mean next weekend when you participate in the assembly at your local church? This is relevant because, in context, Paul was specifically referring to the work of the Holy Spirit in their corporate gatherings. The following verses make immediate application of this filling of the Spirit by saying, "addressing one another in psalms and hymns and spiritual songs, singing and making melody to the Lord with your heart, giving thanks always and for everything to God the Father in the name of our Lord Jesus Christ" (Eph. 5:19–20).

J. I. Packer notes that Paul "describes Spirit-filledness in terms of a lifestyle that all Christians should have been practicing from conversion."[21] Ephesians 5:18–21 indicates that when the Spirit takes control of our hearts we will minister to one another and to the Lord in a variety of expressions as a gathered community.[22]

So rather than our common appeals for the Holy Spirit to

"fall" or bring down some kind of spiritual rain from heaven, our cry should be, "Holy Spirit, take complete control of my mind, my heart, and my will. Show Jesus and His glory to me and through me. Make me keenly aware of His holiness and power in my life. Make me fully responsive to Your Word and will that I might become more like Christ and fulfill His purposes in this world—starting right now in my worship of You and my ministry to those around me." This, in the true new covenant sense, is the filling of the Holy Spirit in our gatherings as the people of Christ. Rather than searching for an outside-in work that might feel more spectacular, we need to embrace an inside-out work that will be ultimately sanctifying.

> **Rather than searching for an outside-in work that might feel more spectacular, we need to embrace an inside-out work that will be ultimately sanctifying.**

SPIRIT-FILLED GATHERINGS

Often we will label a congregation as a "Spirit-filled church" based on certain denominational or behavioral characteristics. It seems helpful for us to align our descriptions with the clear New Testament descriptions of Spirit-controlled worship. Paul's teaching specifically explains the work of the Holy Spirit in corporate gatherings. Gordon Fee points out that the application of the command to be Spirit-filled results in "a community!—whose life is so totally given over to the Spirit that the life and deeds of the Spirit are as obvious in their case as the effects of too much wine are obvious in the other."[23]

A Spirit-filled gathering is described in this way: "Addressing one another in psalms and hymns and spiritual songs, singing and making melody to the Lord with your heart, giving thanks always and for everything to God the Father in the name of our Lord Jesus Christ, submitting to one another out of reverence for Christ" (Eph. 5:19–21). Three outcomes are clear in the text: *Christ-centered singing, Christ-centered gratitude,* and *Christ-centered submission.* Notice all of them have a common point of reference for a Spirit-filled experience—Jesus Christ.

Christ-Centered Singing

In the next chapter we will deal specifically with the role of music in experiencing the transforming presence of the Holy Spirit. But to put it simply, "taken together 'psalms', 'hymns', and 'songs' describe 'the full range of singing which the Spirit prompts.'"[24] Christ-centered singing involves both horizontal and vertical expression. And, all of this flows from the heart—controlled by the indwelling Spirit. "*Heart* here signifies the whole of one's being. The entire person should be filled with songs of praise; thereby expressing the reality of life in the Spirit."[25]

Christ-Centered Gratitude

The filling of the Spirit compels us to "giv[e] thanks always and for everything to God the Father in the name of our Lord Jesus Christ." When we are controlled by the Holy Spirit, who is effecter of the work of Christ in our lives, our hearts agree with Paul's Spirit-filled gratitude: "But thanks be to God, who in Christ always leads us in triumphal procession, and through us spreads the fragrance of the knowledge of him everywhere" (2 Cor. 2:14). Our hearts give gratitude to God, who has blessed us with every spiritual blessing in Christ (Eph. 1:3–14). In worship, our souls cry out, "But thanks be to God, who gives us the victory through our Lord Jesus Christ" (1 Cor. 15:57) and "Thanks be to God for his inexpressible gift!" (2 Cor. 9:15). And we constantly thank God for one another, as Paul so often did in his letters to fellow believers.

Christ-Centered Submission

Spirit-filled worship eliminates pride, position, and any sense of performance that elevates one believer above another. Loving, mutual submission was a theme Paul emphasized to the Corinthian church in 1 Corinthians 12–14. Here again, Christ-centered worship and the inside-out work of the Spirit is so crucial. We submit out of reverence for Christ. We are His willing servants, exhibiting complete submission to Him (2 Cor. 4:5). As true disciples of our Savior, we follow Christ's example of ultimate submission to the will of God in His sacrificial death on our behalf (Matt. 20:28; 26:39; 2 Cor. 8:9; Phil. 2:1–11). "There must be a willingness in the Christian fellowship to serve any, to learn from any, to be corrected by any, regardless of age, sex, class, or any other division."[26] Paul continues his application in Ephesians 5:21–6:9 to show that this Spirit-filled, Christ-reverencing worship will be evidenced in every possible relationship. He gives very specific teaching to wives, husbands, children, fathers, employees, and employers. The highly relational "fruit of the Spirit" (Gal. 5:22–23), which is the overflow of a Spirit-filled life, will change the way we live as we interact with all people.

> **When we reenact old covenant approaches, we end up with a Spirit who comes and goes rather than one who indwells and transforms.**

Arriving at our gatherings with a focused desire for the Spirit to "fill" will transform our lives from the inside out and become the true new covenant "normal" of our Christian experience. When we reenact old covenant approaches, we overshadow new covenant promises and power. We end up with a Spirit who comes and goes rather than one who indwells and transforms. When we pursue ideas that are not taught in the New Testament we may experience moments of temporary inspiration but will fail to experience the promises that produce long-term transformation.

"A congregation learns its theology, and takes it down into the crevices of their soul, by the songs that they sing, not just by the preaching they hear. . . . There is no reason for any church to sing songs that are misleading or even questionable." —JOHN PIPER

"My Christian understanding was largely formed by what I sang because those were the words that stuck with me. We must not underestimate the influence of the songs that we sing. One theologian said once: 'Show me your songs, and I will tell you your theology.' That means that great care must be taken in the choice of songs." —VAUGHAN ROBERTS

FILTER THE MESSAGE IN THE MUSIC

The Indwelling Spirit Inspires Worship That Honors His Truth

I am a music lover. Perhaps it came from my early years of growing up in church. My parents weren't musical, but I do remember some antiquated black-and-white pictures of my older brothers playing the accordion, a pursuit they abandoned quickly (almost as quickly as I abandoned my organ lessons). Still, music is in my soul. I truly cherish many of the good old hymns and gospel treasures.

In high school, I loved choral music (second to football), even singing in "All State Choirs." During those same years I learned to play the guitar and led our campus prayer group in the newly discovered array of "contemporary Christian music." I received a full-ride scholarship my first two years in college by participating on a couple of traveling music groups.

It seems I always have a tune in my head. My church staff often called me "the humming pastor." My wife says I even hum to avoid tense conversations with her. Maybe so.

Ministry colleagues have called me a "Christian jukebox" because I have unusual recall of a vast array of songs. This is most often evidenced in the spontaneous environment of prayer summits where we sing a cappella songs for days at a time. I love my multiple playlists on my smartphone. Even as I have been writing this book, music has been going in the background via Spotify.

All of this is to say, I cherish and am very "tuned in" to music, trends in musicology, and especially the lyrics used in worship services today. I love worship pastors and church musicians, and admire what they do. In today's Christian culture, they exercise incredible influence in how congregations think of and seek to experience the Holy Spirit. So, to embrace the importance of the transforming presence of the Holy Spirit, we must include an honest, and I trust biblical, evaluation of where we are and where we should go in this thing we call worship through song.

THE POWER OF MUSIC

Music is important to us because it is important to God. The Father sings over His people (Zeph. 3:17). Jesus sang (Matt. 26:30; see also Heb. 2:12). One result of being filled with the Spirit of God is singing (Eph. 5:19). Throughout biblical history God's people wrote songs and sang to Him. The Psalms are packed with encouragements to sing and were actually the lyrics of songs that were utilized by God's people. A number of New Testament passages indicate the place of song in the early church (Acts 16:25; 1 Cor. 14:26; Eph. 5:19; Col. 3:16; James 5:13). There is, and will be, music and singing in heaven (Rev. 5:8–11; 14:2–3; 15:1–7).

Music is powerful. The Scottish poet Carlyle is purported to have once said: "Let me make a nation's music, and I care not who makes her laws. I will control that nation."[1] Serge Denisoff, a sociologist at Bowling Green University, said: "If you want to reach young people in this country, write a song, don't buy an ad."[2] Many studies in education, medicine, and other fields show the power of music for effective learning, physical health, and emotional well-being.[3]

When used in Christian experience, music has power to shape our understanding and recollection of truth (or error). We must be careful and vigilant to embrace music as a means by which the Holy Spirit achieves His purpose: to glorify Christ.

MUSIC OVERLOAD

Ron Owens notes that in previous generations of the church, music was primarily written by ministers such as "Isaac Watts, John Newton, and Charles Wesley." Because of their biblical acumen, "their texts were scripturally-based and theologically sound."[4] Most songs were written for the church, primarily to teach solid doctrine and provide biblical application for the encouragement of the saints. Worship songs were designed to serve the church in cherishing the truth and advancing the gospel. There was no concern about record sales, downloads, the popularity of online music videos, or sold-out concerts. This just did not figure into the crafting of music for worship.

We have to be honest and admit that today, worship music is most often produced in the context of an "industry." Song creation, at least in part, is inspired by artists hopeful to secure extraordinary plays on the local Christian stations, lots of downloads, and regular engagement in churches across America, even the world. Often these ambitions are sincere and gospel-centered. Yet some of the larger record labels are owned by secular companies that probably have little concern about the theological accuracy of the music. Sales are king. I suspect this must somehow affect the process of producing a lot of Christian music.

Please know, I am grateful for Christian music. I am a regular consumer and I cherish inspiring songs as I am flying on a plane to speak somewhere, working at my desk, or dozing off at night. These tunes can facilitate real and powerful ministry.

But we must acknowledge that amidst the viral explosion of Christian music there is potential for dilution of biblical truth. Proverbs 10:19 says, "When words are many, transgression is not lacking, but whoever restrains his lips is prudent." I know I need that wisdom for my everyday life, whether it is family conversations, phone calls with staff, my preaching, or my writing. I am sure it is good wisdom for those who create modern worship music as well.

MOTIVATION AND MESSAGE

Of course, no one is able to judge the motives of any particular songwriter. Many whom I have known personally have been deeply spiritual and genuine in their aspirations. The Lord truly led them to what they do and has graciously blessed their ministry. But as Ed Steele has noted, "We really don't sing intentions, but words."[5] He affirms that words have meaning, and when those words are implanted in the heart with catchy melodies they become a part of who we are. I am not urging us to judge

> **Words have meaning, and when those words are implanted in the heart with catchy melodies they become a part of who we are.**

the motives of any songwriter or worship leader but to carefully filter the message in the music. D. A. Carson has made the observation that "many contemporary 'worship leaders' have training in music but none in Bible, theology, history, or the like. When pressed as to the criteria by which they choose their music, many of these leaders finally admit that their criteria oscillate between personal preference and keeping the congregation reasonably happy—scarcely the most profound criteria in the world."[6] Bryan Chapell offers a good word of warning: "If gospel priorities do not determine worship choices, then people's preferences will tear the church apart."[7]

SPIRIT-INSPIRED CREATIVITY

The Holy Spirit, by whose power the world came into creation (Gen. 1:2), is amazingly creative. Through the work of the gospel, He dwells in the heart of every believer in profound power and wisdom (1 Cor. 2:9–13). He has a unique plan for every life. He has truth for every church, as we see in His targeted messages to the churches in Revelation 2–3. Yet Christ tells each assembly, "He who has an ear, let him hear what the Spirit says to the churches."

I am regularly amazed by the creative capacity of the human soul and mind. God made us to express God-inspired originality, evidenced by Adam's divine assignment to name all the animals (Gen. 2:19–20). How long did that take? How many animals were in existence at the time? I wrote about the creativity of God's character, Word, Spirit, and handiwork as it relates to prayer in my book PRAYzing![8] God is honored when mankind is creative. He is marvelously glorified when our creativity advances the gospel and communicates biblical truth.

Today we need creativity that will clarify truth, not confuse it; an artistry that will accentuate the gospel, not obscure it; songs that will declare the wonders of the finished work of Christ, not distract from it. All of these can be uniquely guided by the Holy Spirit from week to week.

> Today we need creativity that will clarify truth, not confuse it; an artistry that will accentuate the gospel, not obscure it; songs that will declare the wonders of the finished work of Christ, not distract from it.

But a distressing downside of the proliferation of Christian music as an "industry" is the tendency to simply imitate or mechanically "plug-and-play" a music set, rather than doing the necessary work of knowing the heart and mind of the Holy Spirit for each church, each gathering, each believer—discerned through diligent time spent in prayer and the Word of God. I think we all want the same thing.

Professor Ed Steele comments, "C. S. Lewis spoke about how dogs generally won't look to what you point at with your finger, instead, they go sniff the finger, missing your intentions. Worship, for many, is like that. They begin to focus on worship itself, rather than the God to whom all worship belongs."[9] He notes that some of the "fingers" are the emotions of worship, style, and structures of music, the individual parts of a service, the personalities of the worship leaders, and even worship itself. I fear that in many cases, the finger is just doing what is popular versus what really reflects a worship of "spirit and truth."

CAREFUL ABOUT WHY WE SING

In recent years, it has become common to view music as the means by which we are "brought into God's presence." One author, representative of this view, explains a view of worship, "It stands to reason that Presence is released. Atmosphere is changed. . . . This is an amazing result from a dove being released. . . . The atmosphere changes as the Presence is given His rightful place."[10] It appears that the goal is to give this "Presence" preeminence through the singing. (For clarification on the idea that God "inhabits the praises of His people" go to transformingpresencebook.com.)

There is no New Testament verse teaching that music is a means of mediating the presence of the Holy Spirit. In some gatherings it appears that the worship leaders are trying to "channel" the Holy Spirit through the music, which is far more akin to mysticism than to biblical Christianity.

As we have seen in previous chapters, music is an expression or overflow of the indwelling Holy Spirit controlling us (Eph. 5:18–19). It is also the "word of Christ" at work in our hearts that gives us cause to sing (Col. 3:16). Bob Kauflin makes an insightful observation at this point: "For those of us who think of worship primarily in terms of musically driven emotional experiences, Jesus' conversation with the Samaritan woman should be eye-opening. Jesus is talking about 'true worshipers' and he doesn't reference music once. Not a whisper of bands, organs, keyboards, choirs, drum sets, guitars, or even lutes, lyres, and timbrels. . . . Music is a part of worshiping God, but it was never meant to be the heart of it."[11]

Speaking about music, Vaughan Roberts clarifies, "It is not the means by which we enter the presence of God, but it is one of the ways in which we can express our joy at the wonderful truth that we are already there, in his presence, in Christ."[12] He also insightfully describes four dangers of viewing "music as an encounter with God."[13] Pete Ward has observed, "Where Catholics or high church Anglicans may see the Eucharist as a place of 'encounter,' and where the Reformed tradition and its offshoots may see the preaching of the Word of God as the place of 'encounter,' the Charismatic tradition sees the singing of praise and worship as the place of encounter."[14] Many have referred to this as the "sacramentalization of singing"—worship singing is the new sacrament. I would add that this is not just a "charismatic" perspective but a growing point of confusion across the spectrum of evangelical Christianity.

> We do not sing in order to be filled with the Holy Spirit. We are filled with the Holy Spirit so that we might sing.

The lyrics of clear biblical truth in music can certainly deepen our worship and positively affect our emotions. (We will unpack the importance of emotion in the next chapter.) But the Bible is clear that it is the work of Christ *alone* that has mediated the presence of the Holy Spirit in our lives. The real concern is that some very confusing songs create false expectations and can lead to a disappointed or misguided faith. Further, any diversion from the truth of what really mediates God's presence (other than Christ) dilutes the glory of the gospel and diminishes the power and truth of all His cross has accomplished for us.

We do not sing in order to be filled with the Holy Spirit. We are filled with the Holy Spirit so that we might sing. The New Testament nowhere teaches that the Holy Spirit works through the medium of notes, sound systems, and tunes to deliver God's presence or enabling the Holy Spirit to take control of our lives. Rather, the Holy Spirit's control in us will produce heartfelt worship expressed in song for the glory of Christ. The truth in the songs can certainly inform and inspire our worship, but the song is not the key to the "Presence."

Michael Horton notes, "Vagueness about the object of our praise inevitably leads to making our own praise the object. Praise therefore becomes an end in itself, and we are caught up in our own 'worship experience' rather than in the God whose character and acts are the only proper focus."[15]

CAREFUL ABOUT WHAT WE SING

Our ministry website (64fellowship.com) is designed specifically for pastors and contains a selection of prayer tools for leaders.[16] Some guides are based on songs frequently featured in evangelical churches. We provide a variety of prayer prompters, in connection with the truths of the songs. The hope is that churches can integrate life-giving prayer moments during the musical worship. As I create this resource on a monthly basis, I have found that some songs are quite difficult, in fact almost impossible, to feature—especially as I seek to find truly biblical ideas to connect to the lyrics in order to help people pray scripturally.

Appendix 2 suggests a new covenant vocabulary. As you read it you will recognize many phrases used in modern worship songs that need to be evaluated in light of the finished work of Christ. Words matter.

CAREFUL ABOUT HOW WE SING

As stated in an earlier chapter, the more sophisticated our tools of ministry have morphed, the greater the danger has grown that the lines of real New Testament worship versus mere entertainment have blurred. I say often when I speak to pastors that, while we have more tools today than at any time in church history, there is nothing inherently wrong with the tools. (The last church I pastored had a 4,200 seat auditorium, all the latest technology, and a multimillion-dollar budget for purchasing the latest gear.) But there is a difference between simply *using* the tools and *trusting* the tools. The test is our genuine understanding of and reliance on the power of the Holy Spirit through earnest prayer.

EXALTATION, NOT ENTERTAINMENT

The *Alliance of Confessing Evangelicals* is a broad coalition of evangelical pastors, scholars, and believers from various denominations. They have coalesced to call the church, amidst a dying culture, to repent of its worldliness, to recover and confess the truth of God's Word, as did the Reformers, and to see that truth embodied in doctrine, worship, and life.

Their first united effort, *The Cambridge Declaration*, emphasizes the importance of regaining adherence to the five "solas" of the Reformation. The Fifth of those declarations, *Soli Deo Gloria* (for the glory of God alone), expressed a concern over the erosion of God-centered worship. Part of that declaration states:

> God does not exist to satisfy human ambitions, cravings,
> the appetite for consumption, or our own private spiritual
> interests. We must focus on God in our worship, rather than

the satisfaction of our personal needs. God is sovereign in worship; we are not. Our concern must be for God's kingdom, not our own empires, popularity, or success. . . . We deny that we can properly glorify God if our worship is confused with entertainment.[17]

Entertainment can be defined as "an activity designed to give pleasure . . . or relaxation to an audience, no matter whether the audience participates passively as in watching opera or a movie, or actively as in games," or as "a show put on for the enjoyment or amusement of others."[18] In today's environment, especially in larger churches, or coliseum-scale Christian concerts, we need real biblical discernment to know the difference between an entertaining experience and a real engagement in Christ-honoring worship.

Tozer again speaks directly: "When the Holy Spirit begins to move, He often uproots many things we have grown accustomed to. He destroys those things we have been resting upon in order that we might come to the point of resting wholly and completely upon Him. Entertainment is not in the scope of the Holy Spirit. Many churches have given way to this attitude of entertainment and as a result have hindered the Holy Spirit from working."[19]

A SHOW OF HIS GLORY?

Today we sing songs about God "showing us His glory." Is it clear what we are hoping for? God's glory is not some level of communal emotion, although His glory can affect us at every level. God's glory is not embedded in the technological stimuli of today's worship environments. God's glory is not about making us feel better about ourselves at some superficial level.

God's glory is awesome beyond imagination and brings the human heart to a place of abject humility, surrender, confession of sin, and uninhibited, self-sacrificing worship. Ron Owens explains that "one of the basic meanings of *to glorify* is to give a correct interpretation of something."[20] Christ is glorified when we correctly interpret His glory.

Now, I love the account of Moses in Exodus 33:18, where he cried out, "Show me your glory." It is hands down my very favorite story of the Old Testament. But today, as Jesus followers, living in the new covenant, we must remember that the finished work of Christ and the New Testament teaching have moved us far beyond any old covenant understanding of glory coming and going, leaving and returning. New covenant glory is not a mysterious passing by or visitation of an external presence as it was with Moses. The glory is *in* us! He has already shown us His glory in the face of Jesus Christ. That is the message of the cross—a message we cannot diminish by our traditions or cherished old covenant lyrics. We can praise God that He *has* and *continues to* show us His glory in Christ.

In applying the new covenant to our lives, Paul writes, "For God, who said, 'Let light shine out of darkness,' has shone *in our hearts* to give the light of the knowledge of the glory of God in the face of Jesus Christ" (2 Cor. 4:6). As Paul wrote this, he had just emphasized our "glory to glory" experience based on the power of the indwelling Spirit (3:18 KJV). He was clear about our experience of "the light of the knowledge of the glory of Christ" through the message of the gospel (4:6).

We do not need to ask God to "show us His glory" as if it is some atmospheric phenomenon. The Bible says, "And the Word became flesh and dwelt among us, and we have seen his glory, glory as of the only Son from the Father, full of grace and truth"

(John 1:14). Hebrews affirms, "He is the radiance of the glory of God and the exact imprint of his nature" (Heb. 1:3). And now, hallelujah, we have the profound reality of the Holy Spirit, the "Spirit of Christ" (Rom. 8:9; 1 Peter 1:11; see also Gal. 4:6), living *in* us. Our confident declaration in all of our worship is, "Christ in you, the hope of glory" (Col. 1:27).

EDIFICATION BEYOND EDUCATION

Experiencing the Spirit in our worship is intricately connected to the Word of Christ. As we've seen in Ephesians 5:18–21, being "filled with the Spirit" is expressed as we address "one another in psalms and hymns and spiritual songs, singing and making melody to the Lord with your heart." Paul wrote in parallel terms to the Colossians with this admonition, "Let the word of Christ dwell in you richly." Spirit and Word. The fruit is the same: "teaching and admonishing one another in all wisdom, singing psalms and hymns and spiritual songs, with thankfulness in your hearts to God (Col. 3:16–17).[21]

> **Horizontally, we minister to one another by applying biblical truth, even through songs. Vertically, we sing and make melody to the Lord, in a spirit of thankfulness.**

This guideline for all of this was given by Paul in 1 Corinthians 14:26, "Let all things be done for building up."

Again, notice both the *horizontal* and *vertical* dimensions of worship that truly "build up." Horizontally, we minister to one another by applying biblical truth, even through songs. Vertically, we sing and make melody to the Lord in a spirit of thankfulness.

As Christians today, we do a lot of the vertical, but typically miss the horizontal. I am reminded again of the prayer summit environment. With only our voices, we sing scores of songs a day, some that contain encouraging truth, as we all face inward, seated in concentric circles. Many of our songs are heartfelt, vertical expressions of praise to God. Others are songs of encouragement or testimony.

I remember we sang an old tune one time based on Philippians 1:6, "He who began a good work in you will bring it to completion." As we sang, we looked across the room and into the faces of one another. It was a new (and a bit disarming) but powerful experience for me; one I've come to cherish because I think it represents the spirit of the verses noted above. Many songs of testimony (like the old hymn *Blessed Assurance* or the newer chorus *Our God Is Greater*) are peppered with personal pronouns like "I, me, my, we, our, us." These can be used appropriately for our mutual encouragement.[22] What would happen if we started singing these to one another in actual interaction next Sunday? Maybe mutual edification would break forth. Maybe a powerful "manifestation of the Spirit" would be more common (as we explained in chapter 6).

Perhaps we need to move beyond our current traditional experience of the Word of Christ. Maybe it is more than just a sermon we listen to or a note sheet we dutifully complete. Colossians 3 seems clear. We need to speak the words of the gospel and the teaching of the Bible *to* one another when we gather. How "radical" is that? Radical indeed in today's spectator culture, but new covenant in essence.

MY CONFESSION, OUR PRAYER

As I close I must confess . . . my engagement in worship has been radically changed because of the truths in this chapter. I find myself not just singing to the Savior above but also communing with the Savior within. The worship is sweeter, deeper, and more intimate. Jesus has so much intended for us through the powerful inside-out experience of the Spirit.

Please know, this is not meant to prompt criticism of your worship leaders. Honor them. Express your love for them. Ask the Lord to draw their hearts and minds more clearly to the glorious truths of the finished work of Christ. Pray for them to be guided by the profound implications of the new covenant.

Let's ask that the gospel will truly "filter the message in the music." May our consistent captivation with the work of Christ change why we sing, what we sing, and how we sing, *so that* we will glorify our Savior as we experience His transforming presence.

"That religion which God requires, and will accept, does not consist in weak, dull, and lifeless wishes, raising us but a little above a state of indifference: God, in his word, greatly insists upon it, that we be in good earnest, 'fervent in spirit,' and our hearts vigorously engaged in religion." —JONATHAN EDWARDS

"One of the ministries of the Spirit of God is to mold the human ability to have emotions into an instrument for the display of Christ's character. A very practical understanding of the Holy Spirit's role relative to our emotions will lead to a deeper understanding of the spiritual life." —DAVID ECKMAN

ENJOY THE GIFT OF BIBLICAL EMOTION

The Indwelling Spirit Empowers Me with Sanctified Affections

S o let me get this on the table right up front. I am a "crier." But lest you think I am a hypersensitive type, I also I love to hunt. I growl like Tim the Tool Man when I harvest and dress a deer. But I tear up during many movies.

Recently, while leading one of our national conferences for church leaders, I choked up every time I tried to give the announcements. My heart was intensely moved by what I saw the Holy Spirit doing in the hearts of pastors from around North America. It affected me deeply. Yet, in daily life, my "gift of mercy" is actually subterranean. Go figure.

Emotions are a gift from God, mysterious and often beautiful. But sometimes, if uncontrolled, they feel like a curse and can poison relationships. I'm getting emotional just thinking about my emotions!

EMOTIONS OR THE HOLY SPIRIT?

I certainly do not have an advanced degree in "emotionology," but I believe a discussion about the work of the Holy Spirit must include a balanced, biblical understanding of our very real and necessary emotions. I've realized that many of our suspicions about those "other" Christians are not so much a rejection of their theology but rather an aversion to how they overly process, or fail to process, their emotions as they experience the Holy Spirit.

One camp is on the more expressive side. Observers wonder if it is really the work of the Spirit or just too much caffeine. Maybe they just manifest an eccentric exhibition of personal dysfunction. Others, it seems, might as well join a society of totem poles, as they don't seem to feel anything at all about matters truly divine and supernatural. In any particular weekend gathering you'll discover a diverse mix of thinkers, feelers, and a segment of the unsure.

The inside-out work of the Holy Spirit helps every believer experience vital, holy emotions that are part of our transformational growth. The indwelling Spirit also helps us control emotions that might, in any way, detract from the glory of Jesus and the edification of others. It could be that those who typically worship from the emotional sidelines (whether overtly "wired" or overly "wary") might be missing a balanced, new covenant experience of the Holy Spirit.

Emotion is a gift from God to help us relate to Him and one another. Our feelings

> **Emotion is a gift from God to help us relate to Him and one another. Our feelings are important to our journey of faith.**

are important to our journey of faith. They make an effective servant but can be an excruciating master. Like any gift, we must understand and steward our emotions so that they are formed by truth and fueled by the Spirit to facilitate the advancement of Christ-honoring purposes.

AN EMOTIONAL GOD?

In many places the Bible demonstrates God's intense compassion (Ex. 33:19; Deut. 13:17; Judg. 2:18; Pss. 103:13, 116:5), joy and delight (Deut. 30:9; Isa. 42:1; 62:4; Jer. 32:41), anger (Ex. 22:24; Deut. 6:14–15; Josh. 7:1; Jer. 7:20; Ezek. 5:13), grief (Gen. 6:6; Eph. 4:30), and love (Deut. 7:7–8; Isa. 43:4; Jer. 31:3; Hos. 11:1; 1 John 4:8). In Isaiah 49:15, the Father communicates His affection for Israel with the imagery of a mother caring deeply for her child, clearly one of the most tender and emotionally charged relationships known to man. Zephaniah 3:17 states that "He will rejoice over you with gladness; he will quiet you by his love; he will exult over you with loud singing." Pastor Brian Borgman explains, "Unless we want to chalk up hundreds of passages as 'figures of speech' and eviscerate God's personhood, we must admit biblically that God has and expresses perfect and holy emotions."[1]

JESUS, OUR EXAMPLE OF EMOTION

Jesus is the "radiance of the glory of God and the exact imprint of his nature" (Heb. 1:3). John said that He has made the Father known (John 1:18). Jesus said, "Whoever has seen me has seen the Father" (John 14:9). Paul wrote, "He is the image of the invisible God" (Col. 1:15).

Like the Father, Jesus demonstrated full range of emotion.[2]

New Testament professor G. Walter Hanson has observed, "The gospel writers paint their portraits of Jesus using a kaleidoscope of brilliant 'emotional' colors. Jesus felt compassion; he was angry, indignant, and consumed with zeal; he was troubled, greatly distressed, very sorrowful, depressed, deeply moved, and grieved; he sighed; he wept and sobbed; he groaned; he was in agony; he was surprised and amazed; he rejoiced very greatly and was full of joy; he greatly desired, and he loved."[3]

THE EMOTIONS OF THE HOLY SPIRIT

The indwelling Holy Spirit is the Spirit of the living God (1 Cor. 2:11–14; 2 Cor. 3:3; Phil. 3:3; 1 Peter 4:14) and the Spirit of Christ (Rom. 8:9; 1 Peter 1:11). Thus, we are indwelt by a God of "perfect and holy emotion."

Hebrews 10:29 speaks of those who "trampled underfoot the Son of God" and have "outraged the Spirit of grace." Ephesians 4:30 describes the Holy Spirit being "grieve[d]," which is a word that conveys intense heartache, sorrow, or distress. In Romans 8:26, we are told "the Spirit himself intercedes for us with groanings too deep for words." Literally, the Spirit "laments" or "sighs" as he identifies with our struggles. James 4:5 tells us, "The Spirit who dwells in us yearns jealously" (NKJV). The Spirit "envies intensely with profound longing and desire for total loyalty and devotion."[4] The Holy Spirit is personal and emotional.

Herbert Lockyer writes, "'Personality . . . is capacity for fellowship. The very quality which was most singularly characteristic of Jesus manifest itself in the Spirit, only more universally, more intimately, more surely.' Being able to think, feel, and will, the Spirit has the capacity for fellowship, which is not possible without personality."[5] The inside-out work of the indwelling

Spirit transforms our emotions, making them truly Christlike. The Spirit empowers us to express emotion in a gospel-advancing fashion to be a blessing to the saved, a witness to the lost, and a warning to the disobedient. In the words of Walter Hansen, "We are not to be merely spellbound by what we see in the emotional Jesus; we are to be unbound by his Spirit so that his life becomes our life, his emotions our emotions, to be 'transformed into his likeness with ever-increasing glory.'"[6]

EMOTIONAL IN THE IMAGE OF GOD

We are made in the image of God and thus able to experience meaningful emotion in ways that no other species of God's creation does (Gen. 1:27). The Bible speaks prolifically about human emotion from Genesis to Revelation, perhaps nowhere more often than in the Psalms, where David and other psalmists came to God with a wide array of emotions. Jesus said, "And you shall love the Lord your God with all your heart and with all your soul and with all your mind and with all your strength" (Mark 12:30).

The apostle Paul wrote openly about his emotions. In Acts 20:31, he testified to the elders from Ephesus that he "did not cease night or day to admonish every one with tears." As he departed their company the account says, "There was much weeping on the part of all; they embrace Paul and kissed him, being sorrowful" because they would not see him again (20:37–38). To the Thessalonians he wrote of his affection for them, like a nursing mother, and his encouragement of them, like a father (1 Thess. 2:7–8, 11–12). In Galatians 4:19, he described his feelings toward the church like the "anguish of childbirth." He spoke openly of his extreme joy and personal longings in connection with the God's people (Phil. 1:8; 4:1; 1 Thess. 2:19-20; 2 Tim. 1:4). In

2 Corinthians, Paul's transparency prompted him to make specific references his emotions no less than thirty-five times![7]

Spiritually healthy people are aware of the vital role of emotion as beings made in the image of God and saints called to transformation into the image of Jesus.

God desires that we express emotion. Brian Borgmans writes, "Another consideration is that God in His Word actually commands us to feel certain ways and express certain emotions. Rejoice, fear, be angry, weep, mourn, delight are all biblical mandates that must not be reduced to mere acts of the will (Philippians 4:4; Matthew 10:28; Ephesians 4:26; Romans 12:15; Psalms 37:4). These commands engage the emotions. Far from being the caboose, the feelings or emotions are a vital part of our humanity which needs to be cultivated through God's Word."[8] As one counselor has noted, "Ignoring our emotions is turning our back on reality; listening to our emotions ushers us into reality. And reality is where we meet God. . . . Emotions are the language of the soul. They are the cry that gives the heart a voice."[9] The great Bible teacher, D. Martyn Lloyd-Jones wrote,

> I regard it as a great part of my calling in the ministry to
> emphasize the priority of the mind and the intellect in
> connection with the faith; but though I maintain that, I
> am equally ready to assert that the feelings, the emotions,
> the sensibilities obviously are of very vital importance. We
> have been made in such a way that. . . . one of the greatest
> problems in our life in this world, not only for Christians,
> but for all people, is the right handling of our feelings and
> emotions. Oh, the havoc that is wrought and the tragedy,
> the misery and the wretchedness that are to be found in the
> world simply because people do not know how to handle

their own feelings! Man is so constituted that the feelings are in this very prominent position, and indeed, there is a very good case for saying that perhaps the final thing which regeneration and the new birth do for us is just to put the mind and the emotions and the will in their right positions.[10]

EMOTIONALLY HUMAN

Emotional reactions are essentially outward expressions of what is going on inwardly. The exuberant happiness I experienced when the Seahawks clobbered the Broncos in Super Bowl XLVIII was only matched by the exasperating disappointment I felt the next year when they gave the victory away to the Patriots in the final minute in Super Bowl XLIX. Emotions are a part of life. Christians and non-Christians alike get emotional about many things: sports, romance, births, deaths, personal conflict, injustice, etc. Raw emotion, prompted by a happy or tragic event, is common to all people and part of the glory of God creating us in His image. Yet only Christians can experience truly holy emotion. Christ-honoring, Christ-witnessing, Christ-loving emotion is unique to those indwelt by the Holy Spirit. Christians also have emotions rooted in the glory of the gospel.

There have been many occasions when I have wept over men expressing deep repentance at a prayer summit. I have cheered joyously at outdoor baptisms and felt profound agony as I've seen the spiritual lostness of people in various nations of the world. I've struggled with deep grief watching my parents and treasured church members slip from this life on their deathbed. I've felt the joy of the angels when someone committed their life to Christ after we've prayed for many years.

Our feelings can be positive or negative, godly or carnal. We know they can tend to change on a dime and are sometimes hard to understand. Several of my godly mentors have advised, "Never let your highs get you too high, or your lows get you too low." Perhaps they knew I had a particular need for this wisdom.

A TOOL OF PURPOSE

So as you think about the inside-out work of the indwelling Holy Spirit, let Him engage and empower your emotions, but also govern them. Writer Jon Bloom counsels:

> God designed your emotions to be gauges, not guides. They're meant to report to you, not dictate to you. The pattern of your emotions (not every caffeine-induced or sleep-deprived one!) will give you a reading on where your hope is because they are wired into what you believe and value—and how much. That's why emotions like delight (Psalm 37:4), affection (Romans 12:10), fear (Luke 12:5), anger (Psalm 37:8), joy (Psalm 5:11), etc., are so important in the Bible. They reveal what your heart loves, trusts, and fears. . . . *pleasure is the measure of your treasure*, because the emotion of pleasure is a gauge that tells you what you love.[11]

Charles Swindoll wrote honestly about his experience of emotion: "I have found that my feelings often represent some of the most sensitive areas in my life touched by the Spirit of God. Not infrequently do my emotions play a vital role in how and where the Spirit is guiding me, giving me reasons to make significant decisions, cautioning me to back off, and reproving me for something in my life that needs immediate attention."[12] Honest and helpful words. He continues, "We are strange creatures: proud of

our brains, stubborn in our wills, but ashamed of our emotions—
though we deny all three!" He states that one of the benefits of a
life sensitive to the Holy Spirit is that it "allows us to warm up to
our emotions, which is nothing more than allowing ourselves the
freedom to be real, to be whole. . . . Expressing one's emotions
is not a mark of immaturity or carnality."[13] The Spirit-inspired
Psalms, packed with emotion of all kinds, affirm and illustrate
this reality.

TRUTH-GUIDED EMOTIONS

Emotions are driven by our thoughts. Circumstances do not
determine our emotions. Rather, our thoughts toward, and in response to, those circumstances drive our emotions. Clearly, there
are real biochemical factors for some people. In some seasons
of life, the weight of a major trial or crisis put us in disarray or
complete brokenness. But most of the time, the emotional battle
is won or lost at the level of our thinking. It's not always what I
am going through but how I am thinking about what I am going
through that sparks strong emotion.

This is where the "renewing of our minds" according to biblical truth is so essential. Ephesians 4:17–24 explains that the
unsaved manifest sensuality and impurity based on hardened
hearts, rooted in the futility of their minds. Believers, embrac-
ing the "truth [that] is in Jesus," are renewed in the spirit of their
minds and able overcome deceitful desires to live out the truth of
a "new self." What we believe fuels how we behave. Lies instigate
destructive feelings. Truth shapes godly reactions and profitable
emotional behavior.

John Piper elaborates with these words: "My feelings are not
God. God is God. My feelings do not define truth. God's word

defines truth. My feelings are echoes and responses to what my mind perceives. And sometimes—many times—my feelings are out of sync with the truth. When that happens—and it happens every day in some measure—I try not to bend the truth to justify my imperfect feelings, but rather, I plead with God: Purify my perceptions of your truth and transform my feelings so that they are in sync with the truth."[14]

HOLY AND HAPPY HEARTS

Tim Keller, advising preachers, writes, "Unless the truth is not only clear but also real to listeners, then people will still fail to obey it. Preaching cannot simply be accurate and sound. It must capture the listeners' interest and imaginations; it must be compelling and penetrate to their hearts."[15] This could also be said about much of our daily communication with family, friends, and work associates. Keller defines the heart as "the seat of the mind, will and emotions all together." He explains that the heart produces emotions, the heart thinks, and the heart wills. He states, "Most fundamentally, the heart puts its trust in things (Proverbs 3:5). Biblically, then, the heart's 'loves' mean much more than emotional affection. What the heart most loves is what it most trusts and commits itself to (Proverbs 23:26). . . . Whatever captures the heart's trust and love also controls the feeling and behavior."[16] He reminds preachers that to preach *to* the heart they must preach *from* the heart and that "sermons may be nothing but good lectures until 'we get to Jesus.'"[17]

This why a biblical view of emotion by church leaders and members is so important. A plaque that has rested on my desk for decades says, "God's word sets me on fire and people come to see me burn."[18] Truth-inspired, godly emotion is contagious in the best of ways. "Worship of God should always involve the emotions; how can we praise a holy God who has redeemed us without getting emotional about it? But what should move our emotions is not the sonorous tones of the organ, or the insistent beat of the drum, but the mind's apprehension of the truth about God."[19]

> **We manage our feelings best when our heart is enthralled with the Savior and we are free to express that love and obedience with our entire being, including emotions.**

Some Christ followers on the road to Emmaus journeyed briefly with the risen Christ. This emotional encounter was recounted with these words: "Did not our hearts burn within us while he talked to us on the road, while he opened to us the Scriptures?" (Luke 24:32). Notice what sparked their spiritual heartburn.

So our emotions are a function of the loves of our heart. The loves of our heart are shaped by the truths we believe. Conversely, our loves can drive our thoughts. In the complicated mix of human emotion, one thing is sure: we are wise when truth shapes our trust. And because the Holy Spirit's purpose is the glory of Jesus, we manage our feelings best when our heart is enthralled with the Savior and we are free to express that love and obedience with our entire being, including emotions.

Dr. David Eckman helps us with an essential distinction: "Emotions do not authenticate truth; emotions cannot verify the historicity of the resurrection of Christ or other historical and theological realities. Emotions, however, do authenticate our understanding of the truth. A happy heart is the greatest evidence of the apprehension of spiritual truth. In the Bible, truth is supposed to strike the life with positive emotional force. Truth without effect is an unknown within scripture."[20]

SPIRIT-ACTIVATED EMOTIONS

The New Testament also shows a profound contrast between those whose lives are guided and oriented around the Holy Spirit and those ruled by their flesh. The fruit of these dissimilar lifestyles is seen in some emotionally infused terms. The flesh is evident in "sexual immorality, impurity, sensuality, idolatry, sorcery, enmity, strife, jealousy, fits of anger, rivalries, dissensions, divisions, envy, drunkenness, orgies, and things like these" (Gal. 5:19–21). Some of these behaviors would be classified as emotional manifestations, the others involve emotional motivations.

But those whose regular conduct is ordered according to the life of the Holy Spirit embrace truth and exhibit trust in ways that demonstrate "love, joy, peace, patience, kindness, goodness, faithfulness, gentleness, self-control" (5:22–23). Our emotions are transformed by the inside-out work of the Holy Spirit.

When we are filled with the Spirit, our truth-based and truly healthy emotions are focused on the astonishing wonder of the person and work of Jesus. The Spirit's control overflows in song, gratitude and willing submission (Eph. 5:18–21). "Theologically speaking, emotions are 'rightly ordered' when they are appropriately directed. In order for an emotion to be considered 'a full-fledged emotion'—as opposed to, say, a 'mood'—it needs an object: something to be directed toward. To have our emotions rightly ordered, then, is to have them appropriately directed toward the right objects."[21] The right and best object is the person, purposes, and power of Christ.

BALANCED EMOTIONS IN THE CHURCH

In some churches, emotion can seem like a narcotic that must be dispensed from the platform each week through various delivery systems. The evaluation of the service as being good or bad, powerful or dull, Spirit-filled or boring is rooted in the level of emotion aroused by those in charge of the program. It appears that a heightened level of feeling is the goal.

In other churches, emotion seems to be an intrusive threat to biblical worship, a dangerous distraction to the true work of the Word of God. The music must not provoke any activity below the neck, and the preaching is clearly targeted exclusively to the head. Reason and intellectual learning are the markers of a godly worship service, and emotion is viewed as a hindrance to the work of the Spirit, who is almost spoken of as if He were concerned exclusively with the mind.

In most cases people are stuck somewhere in the middle and not sure what to think, do, or feel. Author Arturo Azurdia speaks of our vulnerability to a "law of diminishing returns," when we are overly dependent on emotional experience in worship: "The maturing Christian will be consistently impaired if devotion to Jesus Christ is determined by fresh experiences of spiritual ecstasy . . . because one's sensation of being overpowered by God will need to steadily intensify. The ordinary will give way to the unusual. The unusual will surrender to the extreme. The extreme will topple to the ridiculous. Often, the inevitable consequence is spiritual emptiness."[22] As J. I. Packer has noted, the danger of an imbalanced emphasis that leans toward a continual need for an emotional high can result in "Christian-centered instead of . . . Christ-centered" worship.[23]

So we must cultivate a Christlike, Spirit-prompted freedom to feel. Yet we must guard our hearts from simply being excited about excitement, emotional about emotions, or worshiping the feelings of worship. Vaught Roberts strikes this balance, "We should not assume that we have encountered God just because we get emotional. It might simply have been the skill of the musicians or the beauty of the songs that moved us. But please do not conclude from that that we should be wary of all emotion."[24] Ed Steele confirms, "The key is to keep our focus on God as the center of our worship and not the emotions that the music may evoke, lest we find ourselves worshiping the feelings generated by the music more than God. We have freedom of emotional expression but focused on the root source, not the result."[25] Again, the root source is Christ and His glorious gospel.

Spirit-filled churches, then, make much of Jesus and the primacy of the new covenant. This affects our thoughts with inspired truth, which fuels our trust and moves our emotions in attributing all-out worth to Jesus. This is not done in some manipulative cheerleader mode but through a Christ-focused environment where leaders and participants alike pursue the glory of the Son of God, in step with the purpose of the work of the Spirit.

OTHERS-EDIFYING EMOTIONS

When we gather with other believers we have an additional responsibility to steward our emotional expressions. How are my expressed feelings affecting others? Paul established clear guidelines for the worshiping community: "Let all things be done for building up," "the spirits of prophets are subject to prophets," and "all things should be done decently and in order" (1 Cor. 14:26, 32, 40). Any manifestation of emotion that has the intention, or even the effect, of drawing attention to oneself needs to be submitted to the "self-control" of the indwelling Holy Spirit.

Because I am invited to minister in a wide array of church settings, I witness a diverse display of emotion. For me, one of the more curious expressions involves women in flowing clothes, dancing around in front of the

> **The forms that we embrace must be subjected to the Bible and the spiritual leaders of the church, then expressed in a way that heightens the glory of Jesus rather than competes for the attention of our fellow worshipers.**

gathering, waving flags in rather wild whirling. Perhaps this is part of your tradition. For me, it was a distraction from the message of the music and competes with a focus on Christ. (I even got whacked in the head once with a flag pole. That was not edifying.)

The point is simple: God commands us to experience emotion. The forms that we embrace must be subjected to the Bible and the spiritual leaders of the church, then expressed in a way that heightens the glory of Jesus rather than competes for the attention of our fellow worshipers.

FINDING THE BALANCE

We all live each day, and come together each weekend, with real needs. Many of these necessities affect our emotions. Unpredictable circumstances, strained relationships, financial pressure, health difficulties, work conflict, and many more dynamics can trigger difficult feelings within the course of any given week.

To manage these responses, we need to embrace biblical truth, applied by the indwelling Spirit, whose very life is one of holy emotion.

Ed Steele notes, "If we worship God so that our needs are met, we are focusing on ourselves. However, when we really focus on God in worship, somehow in God's grace, He meets our needs; the focus is on Him, not my needs or desires. We aren't to pretend we haven't needs when we come in worship. God invites us to bring our needs to Him."[26] Yes, we bring our needs, including the emotions attached to the those needs, to an ever-sufficient Christ, subjecting our thoughts to His Word and submitting our wills to the control of the indwelling Spirit. The Lord does not scold us for our emotions but desires to sanctify our emotions for His glory.

So, tomorrow as you wake up, and this weekend when you worship, here are some helpful questions to ask:

- Am I aware of and open to my God-given emotions?
- What is prompting this particular emotion?
- What thoughts may be fueling and shaping this emotion?
- Are these thoughts being transformed by the Word of God?
- Based on God's Word, where should I focus my trust?
- Are these emotions consistent with the fruit of the Holy Spirit and submitted to His control?
- How can the Holy Spirit use these emotions to glorify Christ?
- How are these emotions affecting others?

- Is my emotional expression building up others or in some way distracting or discouraging them?

- If my regular emotions are proving to be destructive, how and when will I get outside help to maintain emotional health and spiritual maturity?

Emotional balance will go a long way in our experience of the Holy Spirit. In the fringes of dead-pan tradition or feverish frenzy, we can miss God's intention for our experience of perfect and holy emotion. John Piper gives good advice: "Worship must have heart and worship must have head. Worship must engage your emotions and worship must engage your thoughts. Truth without emotion produces dead orthodoxy and a church full of unspiritual fighters. Emotion without truth produces empty frenzy and cultivates flaky people who reject the discipline of rigorous thought. True worship comes from people who are deeply emotional and who love deep and sound doctrine."[27]

"But when we are really in that power, we shall find this difference: that, whereas before it was hard for us to do the easiest things, now it is easy for us to do the hardest" —A. J. GORDON.

"Of course, our reach can exceed our grasp. Even the way of the eagle in the air is beyond us. Hence, our interpretation of who and what the Spirit is, is inadequate because of our inability to read or to describe our own experiences fully. Of this we can be certain, however: Every believer may know without any doubt whatever the fact of the Spirit's indwelling presence, life-giving energy, and sanctifying power. . . . We can be in perfect agreement as to the fact and power of His indwelling." —HERBERT LOCKYER

MAXIMIZE YOUR NEW COVENANT LIFE PLAN

The Indwelling Holy Spirit Changes Everything from the Inside Out

My first car was a 1964 V-8 Ford Falcon. My parents bought it from my oldest brother for $400. At the time, I thought it was the hottest thing on four wheels—especially after I painted it baby-blue, put cool shag carpet inside, installed Hijacker air shocks, and added a set of baby moon hub caps. I know you must be green with envy.

Fast forward to today: in my frequent travels I now rent brand-new cars dozens of times a year. It is really fun to select any automobile from their row of upscale options—all for the same low price. These cars feature satellite radio, high-quality backup cameras, air-cooled seats, heated steering wheels, superior surround sound, high-tech computerized readings, and of course, that new-car, leather-seat smell.

Imagine, that in spite of these modern advancements, I was still driving my old '64 Falcon every day. While it might be nostalgic, the options would certainly be limited. You would think I'm crazy if I cruised around in that old classic persistently trying to tune in to satellite radio, staring at the dash to find the screen for a modern backup camera, and praying for a miraculous return of that new car smell. A classic Ford is fun but doesn't offer the possibilities of a new model.

Some believers today (maybe more than we realize) are still stuck in an outdated edition when it comes to their expectations and explanations of the Holy Spirit. Something profoundly superior is available—and promised in the new covenant. Yes, the Holy Spirit was real and active in the old covenant. But the fulfillment of His ultimate power has been realized in the finished work of Christ.

> You can wake up every morning, cherish every moment, and experience every day knowing, not just that you are in the presence of God but that the presence of God is in you.

You can wake up every morning, cherish every moment, and experience every day knowing not just that you are in the presence of God but that the presence of God is in you.

YOUR NEW LIFE PLAN

Today, "life plans" are a big deal. Trained "life coaches" facilitate these plans for big money. Clients sense a need for something or someone to help them make better sense of their lives and chart a course for effectiveness. Well, here is good news: the God of the universe has a profound life plan. He has clarified it for you. His divine "coach" lives within you and is a supernatural, ever-present, always-wise guide for a daily experience of ultimate abundance.

Jesus gave His all so that you could and would do so. I hope your clearest thoughts and most careful language will reflect the new, complete, and sufficient model of the gospel. Don't try to drive the old covenant model when new covenant life is available and ready for your enjoyment.

As I stated earlier, this book has not been intended to question your experience of the Holy Spirit, but to challenge you to think of His work more clearly and speak from His Word more biblically so that you can experience His power in your life more fully. If we determine that we will continue to grow in our understanding of, love for, and obedience to the Holy Spirit, the Lord will grant us that blessing.

We can be encouraged by J. I. Packer's insight: "Because God is gracious, he may also deepen our life in the Spirit even when our ideas about this life are nonexistent or quite wrong, provided only that we are truly and wholeheartedly seeking his face and wanting to come closer to him."[1] So, assuming you are with me in a this life-altering pursuit, let me encourage you to embrace three core commitments: *see*, *cultivate*, and *walk*. This is the New Covenant Life Plan.

1) SEE Your Christian Life through the Lens of the New Covenant

A new covenant lens empowers you to read, understand, and apply all that the Bible teaches in view of the completed and sufficient work of Jesus Christ.[2] It's like having a cross on your reading glasses. With this perspective, you will understand the work of the Holy Spirit in light of all Jesus intended and the New Testament instructs. This is a true gospel lifestyle.

2) CULTIVATE a Deepening Appreciation for the Finished Work of Christ

Jesus intends that we comprehend and cherish the wonder of the new covenant through our regular celebration of the Lord's Supper. Paul reiterated the Lord's design for our commemoration in 1 Corinthians 11:23–26.

I've been the pastor of churches that provide the Lord's Supper every weekend and others that do so monthly. Sadly, in many cases, it can become an obligation that we cram in at the end of a service in hopes that it might dovetail with the sermon of the day. I heard the story of one church that simply left those all-in-one plastic bread and juice containers in a paper bag at the end of each aisle, instructing the congregation to take advantage of the option if they felt led to do so at some point during the service.

In too many contexts, we have marginalized this sacred ordinance and have effectively diminished our passionate treasuring of the truths of the new covenant. The spiritual ramifications of this neglect are serious, as Paul noted in 1 Corinthians 11:27–32.

I would compel you to ask the Holy Spirit to make your participation of the Lord's Supper more meaningful. In the introduction, I told of the extended, unrushed experiences of the Lord's Table in the prayer summit environment. This has birthed in me a longing for better, more thoughtful, more regular commemorations and celebrations of the "new covenant" secured for us by the blood of Christ. In communion we treasure the "Giver" and the "Gift." We cherish the sacrifice of Jesus and commune intimately with the gift of his indwelling Spirit. Andrew Murray declared, "If we look carefully at what the New Covenant promises mean, we shall see how the 'Sending, forth of the Spirit of his Son into our hearts' is indeed the consummation and crown of Christ's redeeming work."[3] (For some practical thoughts on how to more meaningfully experience the Lord's Table, go to transformingpresencebook.com.)

Baptism is another ordinance that announces the surpassing glory of the new covenant. This public declaration of new life in Christ, the transformation of a rebellious heart, and the gospel purpose of a redeemed soul is marvelously pictured in believer's baptism. Again, we can tend to blow through this ecclesiastical ceremony without understanding the miracle it represents. Yet the resounding message of the gospel is a communal celebration that the old man is indeed buried with Him in the likeness of His death and a new person is raised to walk in the power of new covenant living. If we could make much more of the institution of baptism, we would think much more of the implications of our new life in Christ.

The Lord's Supper and baptism are not just perfunctory obligations of the church. They are powerful opportunities to think highly, feel deeply, and live confidently in the reality of all Christ has provided for us in the new covenant.

The Lord's Supper and baptism are not just perfunctory obligations of the church. They are powerful opportunities to think highly, feel deeply, and live confidently in the reality of all Christ has provided for us in the new covenant.

3) WALK in the Reality of the Inside-Out Power of the Holy Spirit

Corrie ten Boom wrote, "I have a glove here in my hand. The

glove cannot do anything by itself, but when my hand is in it, it can do many things. True, it is not the glove, but my hand in the glove that acts. We are gloves. It is the Holy Spirit in us who is the hand, who does the job. We have to make room for the hand so that every finger is filled."[4] We are to walk each day in a lifestyle of conscious, consistent dependence on the person of the Holy Spirit so that He can implement His supernatural life plan in and through us.

The old covenant revealed the futility of trying to meet God's standard of righteousness through human effort, without the supernatural, abiding power of the indwelling life of God. The new covenant is about the glory of Jesus Christ, whose substitutionary and perfect sacrifice and glorious resurrection have now trumped the unrighteousness of the human heart by providing forgiveness, renewal, and His very abiding presence to fulfill all the righteous requirements of God. His life in us makes the glove of our earthly existence useful, powerful, fruitful, purposeful, and honoring to Christ. Romans 8:11 describes this astounding reality: "If the Spirit of him who raised Jesus from the dead dwells in you, he who raised Christ Jesus from the dead will also give life to your mortal bodies through his Spirit who dwells *in* you."

The new covenant is not about outward reformation but inward transformation.

So in these final pages, let your heart rejoice in the many ways the indwelling Spirit of God, the very power of resurrection life, changes the way you can live each day.

Inside-Out Regeneration

The Old Testament predictions of a new covenant spoke of God giving us a new heart. His truth would renew lives from the inside out (Ezek. 36:26; Jer. 31:31–34). The new covenant is not about outward reformation but inward transformation. We are saved "by the washing of regeneration and the renewal of the Holy Spirit" (Titus 3:5). Through new birth, the indwelling Spirit comes to a soul dead in sin and creates new life, just as Jesus promised (John 3:1–8). The "Spirit of life" sets us free from "sin and death" (Rom. 8:2). I love the way Michael Horton describes this initial work of the Holy Spirit: "Our first experience of God is with the Holy Spirit. Yet it is he who makes us aware of and unites us to Christ through whom we meet a gracious Father."[5]

Inside-Out Identification

In Christ, we not only get new life but we become a new person. We have a transformed identity.[6] "Therefore, if anyone is in Christ, he is a new creation. The old has passed away; behold, the new has come" (2 Cor. 5:17). We are called and empowered to live in the daily renewal of this "new self" (Col. 3:10) with the assurance that we have been "created after the likeness of God in true righteousness and holiness" (Eph. 4:24). A new covenant lens empowers us to see ourselves as we really are in Christ. Because Christ is in us, our new identity is righteous and holy (Rom. 8:4–10; 2 Cor. 5:12). One of Paul's primary words to describe a Christian is "saint," which means "a holy one." The indwelling Spirit confirms the truth of who we really are, enabling us to overcome insecurities and enjoy a significant life from the core of our new identity.

Among the many descriptions of our identity, none is more evocative than our relationship as children of God, adopted, and communing with the Father. Our intimate cry is "Abba" (Rom. 8:15), and as children we are now heirs with Christ (8:17).

Not only do we have a new understanding of who we are but also of where we belong. The Holy Spirit places us in and unites us with the people of God, the body of Christ, the family of faith. We are each a temple of the Holy Spirit as part of the holy temple of God's people. This assurance of who we are and where we belong redefines our purpose and place in this world.

> **The Holy Spirit places us in and unites us with the people of God, the body of Christ, the family of faith.**

Inside-Out Confirmation

The Holy Spirit gives gracious confirmation of our salvation. The Spirit of Christ within us assures us that we belong to God (Rom. 8:9) and His Spirit continually bears witness with our spirit that we are children of God (8:16). First John 5:12–13 tells us that we can "know that [we] have eternal life" based on the indwelling presence of Christ. "Whoever has the Son has life." The work of the Holy Spirit, explained throughout Romans 8, leads us to this conclusion: "For I am sure that neither death nor life, nor angels nor rulers, nor things present nor things to come, nor powers, nor height nor depth, nor anything else in all creation, will be able to separate us from the love of God in Christ Jesus our Lord" (Rom. 8:38–39).

Inside-Out Preservation

Jesus promised, "I give them eternal life, and they will never perish, and no one will snatch them out of my hand (John 10:28). The indwelling Spirit is the fulfillment of this promise—both in giving us eternal life and by preserving us in our faith. The indwelling Spirit is God's seal of ownership and protection in our hearts as "the guarantee of our inheritance until we acquire possession of it, to the praise of his glory" (Eph. 1:13–14; see also 2 Cor. 1:22; Eph. 4:30).

The Holy Spirit provides another "preserving" influence. Paul told Timothy, "By the Holy Spirit who dwells *within* us, guard the good deposit entrusted to you" (2 Tim. 1:14). The indwelling power of the "Spirit of truth" empowers our enduring commitment to the certainty of the gospel. Jesus prayed similarly, "I have given them your word, and the world has hated them because they are not of the world, just as I am not of the world. I do not ask that you take them out of the world, but that you keep them from the evil one. They are not of the world, just as I am not of the world (John 17:14–16). Indeed, he is able to keep us from stumbling and to make us stand in the presence of His glory blameless with great joy (Jude 1:24).

Inside-Out Sanctification

Having begun the work of salvation, the Holy Spirit also completes the work of sanctification in us. This sanctification sets us apart to God in holiness and purity. "He who began a good work *in* you will bring it to completion at the day of Jesus Christ" (Phil. 1:6). He dwells *in* us "both to will and to work for his good pleasure" (Phil. 2:13).

After the upper room meeting with the disciples where Jesus spoke so ardently of the coming work of the Holy Spirit, He began

His extended prayer to the Father, recorded in John 17. As we saw earlier, in many ways, His prayer was His own intimate intercession for the manifestation of the work of the Spirit in the lives of His followers. Jesus prayed, "Sanctify them in the truth; your word is truth. As you sent me into the world, so I have sent them into the world. And for their sake I consecrate myself, that they also may be sanctified in truth" (John 17:17–19).

The indwelling Holy Spirit empowers us to set our minds on the things of the Spirit (Rom. 8:5) and delivers us from life according to our sinful flesh (Rom. 8:9–13). The abiding Spirit gives us the desire and power to obey the Word of God (1 John 3:24). As we walk in the Spirit's power, step-in-step with Him, we do not fulfill the desires of the flesh (Gal. 5:16–21). The Spirit's commitment to our sanctification is very personal, as we know that He is grieved when we sin (Eph. 4:30). He also convicts us to confess our sin to the Lord so that fellowship is restored (1 John 1:9).

Inside-Out Transformation

The new covenant work of the Holy Spirit in our hearts (2 Cor. 3:1–4:6) now produces inside-out transformation. "And we all, with unveiled face, beholding the glory of the Lord, are being transformed into the same image from one degree of glory to another. For this comes from the Lord who is the Spirit" (2 Cor. 3:18).

The goal of our sanctification is transformation into the image of Jesus Christ. In fact, the indwelling Spirit prays in and through us to give us this assurance, conforming us into Christlikeness (Rom. 8:26–29). The fruit of the Spirit's life in us becomes evident in the Christlike characteristics of "love, joy, peace, patience, kindness, goodness, faithfulness, gentleness, self-control" (Gal. 5:22–23). Imagine the potential of the Spirit's indwelling power to make you more like Jesus day after day, until you see Him face-to-face in eternity. We no longer have to try to change but rather trust Him to change us. We don't seek to earn His favor through human effort but rather abide in Him that He might produce fruit in and through

> **We don't seek to earn His favor through human effort but rather abide in Him that He might produce fruit in and through us.**

us. We don't strive to prove our goodness through religious activities but rather through submission to the indwelling Spirit, who makes us truly good. We no longer have to wonder *if* God can change us but can bask in the wonder that He has, is, and will.

Our transformation will produce Christ-honoring testimony. I am reminded of Martin Luther's account of one of his associates, Andreas Karlstadt. Karlstadt was one of the leaders of the Reformation and bore witness of the transformation of the Holy Spirit. Luther said of him, "He has swallowed the Holy Spirit, feathers and all."[7]

Inside-Out Illumination

Oftentimes we need specific insight and guidance to navigate the complexities and decisions of life. The Holy Spirit is our internal GPS, attuned to the truth and character of God. Because we are sons of God, He has committed to lead us by His Spirit (Rom. 8:14; Gal. 5:18).

The Spirit who inspired the Bible is the promised indwelling teacher to help us understand and apply His perfect wisdom. Jesus assured His followers that the Holy Spirit would teach them all they needed to know, bringing to mind His truth (John

14:26). This anointing of the indwelling Spirit gives us convincing knowledge of Christ and His gospel (1 John 2:20).

Granted, there are times when we do not have specific, clear direction for decisions we must make or problems we have to solve. We must trust the sure promises of the Bible, submit to all that the Holy Spirit has made clear, then proceed in the wisdom He gives us. One thing we do know: it is always His will to make us like Jesus in and through every circumstance.

One of His great works of illumination is in continually helping us to fully understand the love of Christ, for us and in us. We know that "God's love has been poured *into our hearts* through the Holy Spirit who has been given to us" (Rom. 5:5). Paul prayed that through God's Spirit in our "inner being" we "may have strength to comprehend with all the saints what is the breadth and length and height and depth, and to know [experientially, not just cognitively] the love of Christ that surpasses knowledge" so that we "may be filled with all the fullness of God" (Eph. 3:16–19). The Lord wants you to experience the fullness of His life as you allow His Spirit to continually confirm Christ's everlasting love for you.

Inside-Out Manifestation

The glorious gospel and the life of the Spirit is not ours to hoard. We are on mission, both to strengthen the work of the gospel in the church and to spread the word of the gospel through the church.

As we saw in chapter 6, the employment of our God-given gifts fulfills a supernatural mission in the body of Christ. "To each is given the manifestation of the Spirit for the common good" (1 Cor. 12:7). Whatever you believe about spiritual gifts, one thing is clear: God has given this supernatural grace to every believer by the indwelling Holy Spirit, and these gifts are exhibited in a variety of ways (see 1 Cor. 12:4–11; Rom. 12:4–8; 1 Peter 4:10–11). His purpose for this manifestation is "that in everything God may be glorified through Jesus Christ" (1 Peter 4:11).

For many years I called the members of my church "laymen" until I realized that they apparently understood this as a command. I would say "laymen," and they would just lay there—doing nothing. Instead, I began to use the biblical term "saints," which is the right term of true honor and clear responsibility. Every saint is a holy servant. Every member is a minister. Every Christian is a contributor—because we are stewards of the grace of the indwelling Spirit of God.

When we consider our witness to the lost, we must remember that in the new covenant, the Spirit of God has written in our hearts to make us a "letter from Christ" to be "known and read by all" (2 Cor. 3:2–3). Paul goes on to say that our new covenant life in the Spirit authenticates the message of the gospel and enables us, by a manifestation of the truth, to "commend ourselves to everyone's conscience in the sight of God" (2 Cor. 4:2). Our confidence for gospel impact is rooted in knowing that God "has shone in our hearts to give the light of the knowledge of the glory of God in the face of Jesus Christ" (4:6).

While our verbal witness is important, the manifestation of the life of Christ through our transformed lives is primary. I am reminded of Peter and John, who were clearly "uneducated, common men" yet put the Jewish leaders in astonishment because it was evident that "they had been with Jesus" (Acts 4:13). So Paul encourages us with the fact that we have the treasure of the new covenant inhabiting "the unadorned clay pots of our ordinary lives" (MSG) in order "to show that the surpassing power belongs to God and not to us" (2 Cor. 4:7).

Inside-Out Proclamation

We must remember that the Holy Spirit is a witness-bearing Spirit. One of His primary functions in our lives is to empower us to speak boldly of Christ and His gospel (Acts 1:8; 4:33). The early disciples, filled with the Spirit, could not help but speak of what they had "seen and heard" of Jesus (Acts 4:20). Paul's requests for the prayer of God's people focused on the bold declaration of the gospel (Eph. 6:19–20; Col. 4:3–4; 2 Thess. 3:1). He commanded that we "Walk in wisdom toward outsiders, making the best use of the time," and that our "speech always be gracious, seasoned with salt" so that we may know how we ought to answer each person (Col. 4:5–6).

Inside-Out Unification

By baptizing us into the body of Christ (1 Cor. 12:13), the Spirit supernaturally unites us with other believers. He creates the "unity of the Spirit in the bond of peace" (Eph. 4:3), which we are commanded to maintain, as the Spirit controls us and produces godly behavior and relationships. Again, after the great Spirit-focused discourse to His disciples (John 13–16), Jesus prayed "that they may all be one, just as you, Father, are in me, and I in you, that they also may be in us, so that the world may believe that you have sent me. The glory that you have given me I have given to them, that they may be one even as we are one, I in them and you in me, that they may become perfectly one, so that the world may know that you sent me and loved them even as you loved me" (John 17:21–23).

In my ministry, I speak and facilitate renewal events that involve a broad mix of denominational and doctrinal backgrounds. Many events draw a diverse ethnic and age group demographic.

The superficial differences are obvious and the finer nuances of our secondary beliefs could easily become a barrier. But a core commitment to the gospel and the authority of God's Word calls us to supernatural commitment to one another. The Spirit

His transforming presence changes everything from the inside out, ultimately reshaping all of our ambitions and efforts to center on God's glory.

within us is greater than the distinctions among us. We should be reminded that Paul went to great lengths to confront disunity, identifying it as a surefire indicator of carnal people who are not surrendered to the Holy Spirit. He even isolated such division as a violation of the holiness and purity of the church as the temple of the Holy Spirit (1 Cor. 1:10–17; 3:1–23).

Inside-Out Glorification

We come full circle to affirm that the primary purpose of the inside-out work of the Spirit in our lives is the glory of Jesus Christ (John 16:14). Paul described the authentic believer as one who will "worship by the Spirit of God and glory in Christ Jesus and put no confidence in the flesh" (Phil. 3:3). Because we were bought with the price of the blood of Christ, our body is the temple of the Holy Spirit and we are commanded to "glorify God" in our bodies (1 Cor. 6:19–20). His transforming presence changes everything from the inside out, ultimately reshaping all of our ambitions and efforts to center on God's glory.

BEYOND IMAGINATION

Pastor Frank Logsdon wrote, "The Holy Spirit is the Administrator of the divine economy. We deal with Him, else we are out of touch with heaven. We yield to His gracious promptings, or we submerge ourselves in the futility of self-will. We receive of His strength, or we will remain impotent. Our eyes will be unopened; our minds will be unenlightened; our hearts will be unaffected; and our feet will be unled."[8] Conversely, when we clearly understand, and are surrendered to the transforming presence of the indwelling Spirit, we are in touch with heaven. We are set free from self-will to embrace His purposes, by His power. Our minds are divinely enlightened to know Christ and the wonder of His calling. Our hearts are fully alive and our steps are ordered by Him. Imagine the possibilities!

Paul's astounding prayer in Ephesians 3:14–21 encourages a rich experience of the Holy Spirit, as we live our days deeply rooted in the love of Christ. I have always loved the culmination of that prayer. For decades it served as my benediction for every church service. It seems a perfect conclusion for our understanding of the inside-out transforming presence of the Holy Spirit.

Now to him who is able to do far more abundantly than all that we ask or think, according to the power at work *within us*, to him be glory in the church and in Christ Jesus throughout all generations, forever and ever. Amen. (Eph. 3:20–21)

Within us! Abundant, mind-blowing, unimaginable power. Perhaps beyond our biggest prayers. Even surpassing our weightiest, most holy and wonderful thoughts. He works for His glory—just as He did in the past, just as He is in the present, and just as He will in the future. Throughout all generations. Forever and ever. *According to the power at work within us!*

"The work of the Holy Spirit, in renovating and sanctifying the heart, is the glory and hope of the Church." —Samuel Miller

"Revival is not just an idea; still less is it mere emotion or excitement. Revival is ultimately Christ himself, seen, felt, heard, living, active, moving in and through His Body, the Church on earth." —Stephen Olford

Conclusion

PURSUING THE HOPE OF A NEW COVENANT REVIVAL

Not long ago, I was chauffeuring a well-known pastor to the airport after a leadership conference. He has written extensively and is respected by pastors across the world, from a wide variety of theological persuasions.

We wandered onto the topic of revival, speaking affectionately of various individuals and ministries that emphasize that message. Midstream, he nonchalantly inserted a riveting statement: "You know, revival is not even taught in the New Testament." I was stunned. I knew this was in no way a dismissal of our need for prayer or any lack of emphasis on the Holy Spirit. Rather, it was an honest observation from a truth-loving student of the Bible who is not beholden to any particular denomination, philosophy, or stream of church methodology.

For weeks, I could not shake his statement. It began to dawn on me that easily 90 percent of the messages I have heard or the books I have read on "revival" are rooted in teachings and stories from the Old Testament. They were based on God's dealing with His people under the old covenant, prior to all the benefits of the finished work of Christ, the outpouring of the Holy Spirit at Pentecost, and the new reality of the indwelling Holy Spirit in the lives of His children. I began to think about my own sermons on revival. Certainly, they were sincere, passionate, maybe even compelling—but based on the Old Testament. Of course, the Old Testament provides many powerful and applicable truths for daily living, especially as they parallel with new covenant teaching.

After a careful search, it was confirmed. I could not find the word "revival" in the New Testament. At best, the concept could be extrapolated from a few indistinct passages.[1] So I again was called to an honest evaluation of much of what I have said, taught, and written, not just on the work of the Holy Spirit, but about the whole idea of revival.

MEANINGFUL BUT MISSING

To be "revived" is "to return to consciousness or life" and "become active or flourishing again."[2] Concerning the actual word "revival," Bill Hull has noted,

> The word is thrown around as if we all know what it means. There is a consensus across the theological spectrum that revival means to fully experience the fulfillment of both the Great Commandment and that the Great Commission, but expectations and descriptions of the revival manifestations vary greatly. . . . Revival is simply a term we have given to the special activity of God throughout history. . . . Spiritual revival (the idea) is in the Bible. Being radically transformed by the power of God based on the finished work of the

resurrected Christ is in the Bible. Whatever it is called, revived, renewed, refreshed, regenerated, liberated, empowered, filled, raised, or healed, I'm for it![3]

Certainly we can agree. We are for all that God wants to do for us, in us and through us by His Spirit. This is what drives our deep interest in "revival." But, as we have seen, the New Testament describes the work of the Spirit in clear terms. His work requires our surrender, obedience, and passion for the glory of Jesus. I've had to remind myself over the years that I cannot prescribe His work by my preconditioned notions, nor can I overzealously promote His work with words that are not in His vocabulary. Bill Hull concurs:

> It is dangerous to give the variety of spiritual experiences in Scripture one label, namely "revival" and then canonize it as the only hope for the church, the nation, and all of humankind. This leads to reliance on God to do all the work – not only his but ours. All spiritual work is God's work, I know that, but Jesus left over 200 commands for his church. Our desperation for revival as a solution is in part evidence of our failure to walk daily in the power of the Spirit and to obey what God has already paid for and equipped us to do.[4]

Iain Murray wrote, "It may be argued that any attempt to define revival is pointless for the word itself is not scriptural and . . . 'may not be wisely chosen.' But rightly or wrongly, it *was* chosen and its sense was commonly recognized over a long period of time."[5] Yet Murray did go to on to describe this work for which we pray as "an extraordinary communication of the Spirit of God, a superabundance of the Spirit's operations, an enlargement of his manifest power."[6]

Richard Owen Roberts has a similar idea of revival: "An extraordinary movement of the Holy Spirit producing extraordinary results."[7] As you might guess, I would like to augment that with a clear new covenant nuance: "An extraordinary movement of the *INDWELLING* Holy Spirit producing extraordinary results."

THE NEW COVENANT AMBITION FOR REVIVAL

From a purely New Testament standpoint, could it be that the "revival" we long for and labor over is essentially an extraordinary sensitivity, surrender, and obedience to the Holy Spirit? I wonder what would happen if we even began to change our language and vocabulary about "revival" and instead emphasized the Christ-glorifying and transformational work of the Holy Spirit in our lives. As Norman Grubb has stated, "Indeed, revival is really just obeying the Holy Spirit."[8] Ultimately, we all can agree to pray for an exceptional movement of the *indwelling* Holy Spirit. We can all pursue an extraordinary obedience to the promptings of the Spirit.

So, believing the truths about the Holy Spirit discussed in this book, and that Christ's sufficient redemption has provided the unspeakable blessing of the supernatural and sufficient Spirit of God in our lives—*then* the Spirit's promises and presence must become the focus of our desire for a fresh work of God. Quoting Grubb again, "The truth is

Could it be that the "revival" we long for and labor over is essentially an extraordinary sensitivity, surrender, and obedience to the Holy Spirit?

that revival is really *the Reviver in action,* and He came two thousand years ago at Pentecost. Revival is not so much a vertical outpouring from heaven (for the Reviver is *already* here in His temple, the bodies of the redeemed) as it is a horizontal outmoving of the Reviver through these temples into the world. It is a *horizontal* rather than a *vertical* movement."[9] Grubb agrees that we should seek an "inside out" experience that moves from heart to heart and life to life in the church, rather than something that falls from heaven when we meet certain conditions or create certain environments.

Grubb describes the reviving work of the Spirit so clearly. He notes that that all Christians relationships are both vertical and horizontal. He proposes that revival incorporates continued two-way brokenness. Vertically, we must be careful to keep "the roof off between ourselves and God through repentance and faith."[10] Horizontally, we must also let the walls come down between ourselves and others. Our walls of pride, self-esteem, and self-respect must be leveled by transparent confession of broken relationships, harbored sin, and pretending to be better than we are.

James 5:16 is clear about the power of this kind of honesty, confession, and believing prayer for one another: "Therefore, confess your sins to one another and pray for one another, that you may be healed. The prayer of a righteous person has great power as it is working." In revival, Spirit-filled Christians testify to one another about the great work of Jesus in their lives. They walk in the light as He is in the light. Roof off. Walls down. Continuous revival.

THE NEW COVENANT
ACCESSIBILITY OF REVIVAL

In my study of the revivals of history, I am convinced that people were not seeking "revival." Most of what I have observed about

revival was the result of common people seeking God for an uncommon work of the indwelling Holy Spirit. It advanced dynami-
cally through heartfelt radical obedience to the Word of God,
resulting in surrender, repentance, and fresh, believing faith. The
gospel was always central. Christ's honor was always paramount.

Accordingly, it is probably not ideal for us to expect any
person or organization to broker revival for the rest of us through
events or prescribed "movements"—including the ministry that
I lead. When we speak of the power of a spiritual re-enlivening
as something that may or may not be attainable by the person in
the pew, we diminish the sufficiency of the truth of the indwelling Christ in every heart. D. Martyn Lloyd-Jones has written,
"Read the story of any revival that has ever taken place and you
will find that the beginning of it is always the same. One man,
or sometimes a number of people, suddenly become alive to the
true Christian life, and others begin to pay attention to them. . . .
that is why our condition as believers is so important."[11]

If we could look at the history of revival, and the various wide-
reaching descriptions through a clear new covenant lens, it would
not devalue the wonder of these profound works of the Holy
Spirit. We never want to diminish or doubt what the Holy Spirit
can do. As Jim Cymbala has reflected, "I never want to let fear of
the unexpected cause me to institutionalize lukewarmness."[12]

Rather, this lens would focus us toward a clearer interpretation of the cause of revival, rooted in the supernatural work of the
indwelling Spirit. This, I believe, would put the idea of revival on
the bottom shelf for every believer. Rather than something unclear and unreachable—an experience that can only be ushered
in by a few gifted professionals—revival would be available to
every believer as they bask in the supremacy of Jesus Christ and
live daily in the sufficiency of the indwelling Holy Spirit. We need

a heightened view and grander expectation of the transforming presence of the Spirit in the heart of every believer.

POSSESSED BY THE REVIVER

We often refer to the glory of "revival" as if it is some amorphous power that invades the church. But the New Testament is clear. To live abundantly, victoriously, and continually—is Christ (Phil. 1:21; Gal. 2:20; Col. 3:4). To experience glory "is Christ in [us], the hope of glory" (Col. 1:27). New covenant life is the transformation of our hearts, described as the "light of the knowledge of the glory of God in the face of Jesus Christ" (2 Cor. 4:6). His "glory in the church" is rooted in the power of that works *in* us (Eph. 3:20–21). Stephen Olford writes, "When by His Spirit He dwells in us in revival fullness all flesh can see the glory of God."[13]

The devil loves nothing more than to distract us from the sufficiency of the gospel. He seeks to diminish our confidence in the Spirit that raised Christ from the dead, who now indwells us in His fullness. Today, many of our promotions are well-meaning and good. But we must guard ourselves from going after an ambiguous event rather than pursuing an abiding empowerment. We should not place our hope in some remote possibility but rather in an assured promise. Emphasizing an atmospheric transaction rather than an internal transformation is a distraction that can lead to spiritual disappointment.

EVERYDAY REVIVAL

Quoting Norman Grubb again, "Revival in its truest sense is an everyday affair right down within the reach of everyday folk—to be experienced each day in our hearts, homes, churches and fields of service.

When revival does burst forth in greater and more public ways, thank God! But meanwhile we should see to it that we are being ourselves constantly revived persons . . . which, of course, also means that others are getting revived in our own circles. By this means God can have channels of revival by the thousands in all the churches of the world!"[14]

I love that! "Channels of revival by the thousands." This includes you and me. This invites every member of your family, your church, your small group into an experience of the indwelling Holy Spirit that is deeper and broader than any of our efforts to organize or promote a new work of God. This calls every pastor to be intentional in facilitating this kind of work in each church. This, I believe, can be the account of our moment in history. The transforming presence of the Holy Spirit is available and sufficient for every Christian and produces radical, unstoppable gospel transformation—in us, through us, and beyond us.

> **The transforming presence of the Holy Spirit is available and sufficient for every Christian and produces radical, unstoppable gospel transformation—in us, through us, and beyond us.**

Olford concurs, "One of the determining factors in seeing a church-wide revival is the determination to fulfill all of God's purposes righteously in the power of the Holy Spirit."[15] As we teach passionately on the clear purposes of the Holy Spirit and surrender fully to His will, a new display of His power in the church, and through the church to the world, can unfold. Robert E. Coleman noted, "In as much as all of us were made to glorify God, revival simply fulfills his desire that we might know him in the fullness of the Spirit and declare his praise to the ends of the earth."[16] I close with these clear and compelling words from Andrew Murray, praying that you will have new and profound faith in the transforming presence of the Spirit of God, in you and through you. I pray you will live in the power of the new covenant, secured, once and for all, by our glorious Lord and Savior Jesus Christ.

I have been very deeply impressed with one thought. It is, that our prayer for the mighty working of the Holy Spirit through us and around us can only be powerfully answered as *His indwelling in every believer* is more clearly acknowledged and lived out. We have the Holy Spirit within us; only he who is faithful in the lesser will receive the greater. As we first yield ourselves to be led by the Spirit, to confess His presence in us, as believers rise to realize and accept His guidance in all their daily life, will our God be willing to entrust to us larger measures of His mighty workings. If we give ourselves entirely into His power, as our life, ruling within us, He will give Himself to us in taking a more complete possession, to work through us.

. . . it is as an indwelling life that Holy Spirit must be known. In a living, adoring faith, the indwelling must be accepted and treasured until it becomes part of the consciousness of the new man: The Holy Spirit possesses me.[17]

FOR MORE PRACTICAL
APPLICATION OF THE
PRINCIPLES IN THIS BOOK
FOR INDIVIDUAL CHRISTIANS,
WORSHIP LEADERS, AND
PASTORS, GO TO

www.transformingpresencebook.com

Appendix 1

ACCURATELY APPLYING THE ACTIONS OF ACTS

The books of the Bible have helpfully been identified with certain primary purposes. For example, the Old Testament is composed of books of law (also known at the Pentateuch—Genesis to Deuteronomy), history (Joshua to Esther), wisdom/poetry (Job to Song of Solomon, also Lamentations), and prophecy (Isaiah to Malachi). Some books contain more than one primary emphasis, like Genesis and Exodus, which also provide significant historical accounts.

In the New Testament, the Gospels and Acts are historical books. They certainly contain some profound teaching (like the words of Jesus and the sermons of Peter, Stephen, and Paul) but are primarily accounts of the life of Christ and the unique work of the Spirit in and through the early church as it was being established, prior to the completion of the teaching of the New Testament.

The letters of Paul (Romans to Philemon) and books written by other New Testament authors (Hebrews to 3 John) are considered teaching or doctrinal books. Revelation is unique, often labeled as apocalyptic, as it primarily provides narrative about things to come in the future.

The Acts of the Holy Spirit in and through the early church is a glorious story of the advancement of the gospel through believers living in the power of the new covenant. The obedience of these early Christians brought great glory to Jesus as the Holy Spirit's power worked in common, and very uncommon, ways to advance the mission of our Lord.

One of the helpful principles I learned early in my pastoral ministry as I studied Acts was to be earnest to experience the teachings of Acts but cautious to teach the experiences of Acts. Bible scholars often make the distinction between "descriptive" passages and "prescriptive" passages. Descriptive passages express events or experiences that definitely happened but are nowhere taught as commands or normative expectations for today's Christian. Prescriptive passages provide vital instruction for Christian living. These prescriptive principles are also confirmed by comparing Scripture with Scripture via the other teaching books of the New Testament.

In the Old Testament, a few examples of descriptive passages might be the stories of Moses before the burning bush, the parting of the Red Sea, the earth swallowing thousands of rebellions leaders, the walls of a city falling flat in response to the blowing of trumpets, the sun standing still, a large fish swallowing Jonah, three men being unscathed in a furnace, a prophet cooking his food over dung and laying on his left side for a year, and another prophet being commanded to marry a harlot. There are many more. These are not to be viewed as prescriptive for the people of God.

In Acts, descriptive passages include the appearance of a mighty rushing wind, tongues of fire in the sky, people dropping dead after lying about their giving, others being healed by a passing shadow, a sheet falling from heaven as a sign to Peter, Phillip being suddenly transported from one location to another, earthquakes opening prison doors, and more. Certainly, God is a miraculous God, but we are not told to instruct or seek to imitate these occurrences.

Many unusual teachings and extrabiblical behaviors have resulted from people trying to make a "descriptive" experience into a "prescriptive" expectation.

On the other hand, prescriptive passages in Acts would include the various sermons and the embedded commands to believe the gospel. Another prescriptive example is Paul's challenge to the Ephesian elders in Acts 20:17–38, where he instructs them about their leadership role. These truths are confirmed in other places in the New Testament.

I think you get the picture. Many unusual teachings and extrabiblical behaviors have resulted from people trying to make a "descriptive" experience into a "prescriptive" expectation. This approach to the Bible truly opens a spiritual Pandora's box that creates massive confusion, great disappointments, and fringe sects. It has been noted that most of our modern arguments stem from the book of Acts.

So what is the key to knowing what portions of Acts are to be authoritative for believers today? The key is to identify clear New Testament commands or repeated teaching passages that indicate a standard for Christian living. Otherwise, we can drift into various forms of legalism or confusing add-on pursuits. Some even fall into a spiritual depression: "Why not me, Lord?"

I define legalism as "creating false standards of spirituality, then judging others by those standards." Legalists treat noncompliant folks as inferior. They concoct rules for real godliness that are not clearly commanded in the Bible. I often note that when someone turns a biblical commentary into a command, they err. When we take the description of an incident and make it a decree of instruction, we lead people astray.

Theologians Gordon D. Fee and Douglas Stuart have summarized it this way: "Unless Scripture explicitly tells us we must do something, what is only narrative or described does not function in a normative way."

They provide helpful guidelines to help us understand what should be considered God's word *for us* in any given narrative:

1) Determining what is normative for Christians is related primarily to what the narrative was intended to teach.

2) What is incidental to the intent must not become primary.

3) For historical precedent to have normative value it must be related to intent.

Furthermore, they propose three specific principles that help us determine whether a narrative in Acts functions descriptively or prescriptively:

1) It is probably never valid to use an analogy based on biblical precedent to give biblical authority to present-day actions.

2) Biblical narratives can have illustrative and "pattern value," even if it may not have been the author's primary purpose.

3) Regarding Christian experience and practice, biblical precedents may be considered *repeatable patterns*, even if they aren't normative. But it is moot to argue all Christians *must* repeat the pattern or they are disobeying God's Word.[1]

Scholar J. B. Polhill notes: "As throughout Acts, there is no set pattern. The Spirit came at various times and in various ways. What is consistent is that the Spirit is always a vital part of one's initial commitment to Christ and a mark of every believer."[2] Today, with the completed New Testament, we are blessed with clear and compelling commands that help us understand the optimal Christian life and the definitive work of the Holy Spirit in every Christ follower.

Appendix 2

A NEW COVENANT
WORSHIP VOCABULARY

S cottish New Testament scholar I. H. Marshall once noted, "Christians are adept at the loose use of language."[1] Throughout this book, I have offered what I believe are some essential correctives in how we speak about the work of the Holy Spirit. I hope these clarifications have been helpful to you—particularly if you believe that the gospel changes everything, that the finished work of Christ is monumental, that the new covenant is important, and that words matter. Martin Sanders, CEO of YouthScape, once tweeted, "If worship is an act of total devotion, then it demands our minds as well as our hearts."

While discussing this book project with a theologically astute president of a Midwestern Bible college, he was somewhat astounded by my thesis. He admitted that what I was proposing was correct but that he, and many of us, would need to be more careful about how we typically speak about the work of the Holy Spirit. He suggested the clarification of a better vocabulary. So, with the belief that such a recommendation is profitable, here it is:

INSTEAD OF:	HOW ABOUT:
"Lord, we welcome You."	"Lord, we are grateful for Your indwelling presence" or "Thank You for welcoming us at the cross."
"We just want to soak in the Holy Spirit."	"Lord, enable us to cherish, honor, and obey the indwelling Holy Spirit."
"The Holy Spirit came."	"The Holy Spirit worked powerfully in our lives."
"We seek Your manifest presence."	"We surrender completely to Your indwelling presence and trust you to use us in one another's lives as we obey the Holy Spirit."
"Release Your Spirit."	"Bring us into complete submission and responsiveness to Your Spirit."
"Holy Spirit fall."	"Holy Spirit fill, control, dominate our lives."
"Pour out Your Spirit."	"Take charge of our lives as we submit to Your indwelling Spirit."
"Fill this temple."	"Fill our hearts."
"God showed up."	"The Spirit worked powerfully in us and among us."
"Welcome to the house of the Lord."	"Welcome to this gathering of God's people."
"This is the house of the Lord."	"You are the house of the Lord, indwelt by His Spirit."

"Flood the atmosphere."	"Take control of our hearts."
"The atmosphere is changing."	"The Holy Spirit is working in us to change us."
"Let Your glory fall."	"Jesus, You are our glory. We seek Your will and word."
"Let our praises fill this temple."	"May the indwelling Spirit inspire our praises."
"Rain down on us."	"Take control of our hearts by Your indwelling Spirit."
"The Spirit of the Lord is in this place."	"The Spirit of the Lord indwells our hearts."
"Thank You that we can come into Your presence."	"Thank You that Your presence has come into us—through the work of Christ."
"We want to attract the presence of the Lord."	"We want to be controlled by the indwelling Spirit of the Lord"
"Blow upon us."	"Work within us."
"When You come into the room."	"When we surrender to Your indwelling presence."
"The Holy Spirit was thick."	"Our surrender and obedience to the power of the Holy Spirit was evident."
"Spirit flood this place."	"Spirit, we surrender our lives to You."
"Reign in this place."	"Have full control of our hearts."

NOTES

Book Epigraph 2: Adolph Saphir, *The Lord's Prayer* (Waikato, New Zealand: Titus Books, 2013), loc. 1567 of 3793, Kindle.

Introduction: What We All Want

Epigraph 1: Francis Chan, *Forgotten God* (Colorado Springs: David C. Cook, 2009), 17.

Epigraph 2: Andrew Murray, *The Spirit of Christ* (Minneapolis: Bethany House, 1979), 6.

1. Judy Woodruff, "Millennials haven't forgotten spirituality, they're just looking for new venues", March 3, 2017, in *PBS Newshour*, produced by PBS, podcast, https://www.pbs.org/newshour/show/millennials-havent-forgotten-spirituality-theyre-just-looking-new-venues.
2. Kari Paul, "Merry Christmas! Why millennials are ditching religion for witchcraft and astrology", MarketWatch, December 19, 2017, https://www.marketwatch.com/story/why-millennials-are-ditching-religion-forwitchcraft-and-astrology-2017-10-20.
3. Jim Cymbala, *Spirit Rising* (Grand Rapids: Zondervan, 2012), 17.

Practice 1: Agree to Evaluate Your Assumptions

Epigraph 1: Charles R. Swindoll, *Flying Closer to the Flame* (Dallas: Word, 1993), 13.

Epigraph 2: Michael Green, *I Believe in the Holy Spirit* (Grand Rapids: Eerdmans, 1975), 11.

1. David Peterson, *Engaging with God: A Biblical Theology of Worship* (Downers Grove, IL: IVP, 1992), 15.
2. Michael Horton, *Rediscovering the Holy Spirit* (Grand Rapids: Zondervan, 2017), 251.
3. "Most American Christians Do Not Believe that Satan or the Holy Spirit Exist," Barna, April 13, 2009, https://www.barna.com/research/most-american-christians-do-not-believe-that-satan-or-the-holy-spirit-exist/.
4. Gordon D. Fee, "Hermeneutics and Historical Precedent—A Major Problem in Pentecostal Hermeneutics," in *Perspectives on the New Pentecostalism* (Grand Rapids: Baker, 1976), 122.
5. Ron Owens with Jenny McMurray, *Return to Worship: A God-Centered Approach* (Nashville: Broadman and Holman Publishers, 1999), 54.
6. Ibid., 147.
7. Charles Haddon Spurgeon, *The Unknown God: 25 Sermons on the Subject of the Holy Spirit* (Aurora, IL: Fox River Press, 2003), 272.
8. Warren Wiersbe, *Real Worship* (Grand Rapids: Baker, 2000), 11.
9 Francis Chan, *Forgotten God* (Colorado Springs, CO: David C. Cook, 2009), 46–47.
10. Robert P. Lightner, *Speaking in Tongues and Divine Healing* (Des Plaines, IL: Regular Baptist, 1965), 7.
11. Andrew Murray, *The Spirit of Christ* (Minneapolis: Bethany House, 1979), 57.

Practice 2: Embrace the Spirit's Primary Purpose
Epigraph 1: Attributed to Charles Spurgeon, http://beggarsallreformation.blogspot
.com/2012/03/spurgeon-i-looked-at-christ-and-dove-of.html.
Epigraph 2: David Ravenhill, "A Word of Caution" last modified April 9, 2012.
https://www.charismamag.com/blogs/prophetic-insight/15067-a-word-
of-caution.
1. Westminster Shorter Catechism, Center for Reformed Theology and Apologetics,
http://www.reformed.org/documents/wsc/index.html?_top=http://www
.reformed.org/documents/WSC.html.
2. D. A. Carson, *The Gospel According to John* (Leicester, England; Grand Rapids:
Inter-Varsity Press; W.B. Eerdmans; 1991), 541.
3. A. B. Simpson, *When the Comforter Came* (Harrisburg, PA: Christian Publications, 1911), 4.
4. J. I. Packer, *Keep in Step with the Spirit* (Old Tappen, NJ; Fleming H. Revell,
1984), 66.
5. Michael Horton, *Rediscovering the Holy Spirit: God's Perfecting Presence in Creation, Redemption, and Everyday Life* (Grand Rapids: Zondervan, 2017), 27.
6. Michael Green, *I Believe in the Holy Spirit* (Grand Rapids: Eerdmans, 1975), 39.
7. Boyd Hunt, *Redeemed! Eschatological Redemption and the Kingdom of God* (Nashville: Broadman & Holman Publishers, 1993), 36–37.
8. Jim Cymbala, *Spirit Rising: Tapping into the Power of the Holy Spirit* (Grand Rapids: Zondervan, 2012), 57.
9. Gordon D. Fee, *God's Empowering Presence: The Holy Spirit in the Letters of Paul*
(Peabody, MA: Hendrickson Publishers, 1994), 157–58.
10. Francis Chan, *Forgotten God* (Colorado Springs: David C. Cook, 2009), 87, 93.
11. A. W. Tozer, *Alive in the Spirit* (Minneapolis: Bethany House, 2016), 111.
12. Eliza E. Hewitt, published 1887, public domain. The last stanza quoted is the
chorus.

Practice 3: Live in the Power of the New Covenant
Epigraph 1: Jim Cymbala, *Storm: Hearing Jesus for the Times We Live In* (Grand
Rapids: Zondervan, 2014), 157. Cymbala is describing the legalistic church
background in which he grew up.
Epigraph 2: Carl B. Hoch, Jr., *All Things New* (Grand Rapids: Baker, 1995), 116.
1. Andrew Murray, *The Two Covenants* (Wellington, South Africa: Andrew Murray,
1898), 10–11.
2. Ibid., 12.
3. D. A. Carson, *Worship by the Book* (Grand Rapids: Zondervan, 2002), 37.
4. The Westminster Confession of Faith states, "The first covenant made with man
was a covenant of works, wherein life was promised to Adam, and in him to his
posterity, upon condition of perfect and personal obedience. Man, by his Fall,
having made himself incapable of life by that covenant, the Lord was pleased to
make a second, commonly called the covenant of grace: wherein he freely offered
unto sinners life and salvation by Jesus Christ, requiring of the faith in him, that
they may be saved, and promising to give unto all those that are ordained unto
life, his Holy Spirit, to make them willing and able to believe." (The Westminster
Confession of Faith, chap. 7, paragraphs 2–3, as found in the *Book of Confessions*,
128–29)
5. Paul R. Williamson, *Sealed with an Oath: Covenant in God's Unfolding Purpose*, NSBT 23 (Downers Grove, IL: IVP Academic, 2007), 43.

6. In biblical times we see covenants that were sealed by an animal sacrifice followed in conjunction with a covenant meal between the parties. Exodus 24:11 gives an example of this as God invited seventy elders up on the mountain and "they saw God, and they ate and drank" (NKJV). Other examples include Isaac and Abimelech (Gen. 26:30), Laban and Jacob (Gen. 31:46, 53–54); and Moses, the Israelites, and Jethro (Ex. 18:12). Participating in these fellowship offerings in the presence of the God likely also included the idea of peace between all parties (Deut. 27:7).

7. D. F. Estes, "Covenant (in the NT)," (1915), in J. Orr, J. L. Nuelsen, E. Y. Mullins, & M. O. Evans, eds., *The International Standard Bible Encyclopedia*, vol. 1–5 (Chicago: The Howard-Severance Company, 1915), 729.

8. Bruce Waltke, "Evangelical Spirituality: A Biblical Scholar's Perspective," *Journal of the Evangelical Theological Society* 31, no. 1 (March 1988): 21.

9. The application of the new covenant in relationship to God's dealings with Israel is a hotly debated topic, particularly between "dispensational theologians" and "covenant theologians." This is a complex study that will not be addressed in this book. For a detailed discussion I would recommend Larry Pettegrew's book, *The New Covenant Ministry of the Holy Spirit* (Grand Rapids: Kregel Publications, 2001).

10. Gordon Fee, *God's Empowering Presence: The Holy Spirit in the Letters of Paul* (Peabody, MA: Hendrickson Publishers, 1994), 297, 301.

11. Carl B. Hoch, Jr., *All Things New: The Significance of Newness in Biblical Theology* (Grand Rapids: Baker, 1995), 122.

12. Jim Cymbala, *Storm: Hearing Jesus for the Times We Live In* (Grand Rapids: Zondervan, 2014), 157.

13. Ibid., 153. Admittedly, this is a point of contention for some. In seminary circles, debates between covenant theology, new covenant theology, and dispensational theology run strong. I am not trying to land in any particular camp, but simply making the point of the superiority of the new covenant. For a good summary of the various views see: Matt Perman, "What does John Piper believe about dispensationalism, covenant theology, and new covenant theology?," Desiring God, January 23, 2006, https://www.desiringgod.org/articles/what-does-john-piper-believe-about-dispensationalism-covenant-theology-and-new-covenant-theology.

14. J. I. Packer, *Keep in Step with the Spirit* (Old Tappen, NJ; Fleming H. Revell, 1984), 59.

15. Carol Kern Stockhausen, *Moses' Veil and the Glory of the New Covenant* (Rome: Biblical Institute Press, 1989), 105.

Practice 4: Pursue the Indwelling Person, Not an External "Presence"

Epigraph 1: Michael Horton, *Rediscovering the Holy Spirit: God's Perfecting Presence in Creation*, Redemption, and Everyday Life (Grand Rapids: Zondervan, 2017), 20.

Epigraph 2: R.A. Torrey, *The R.A. Torrey Collection*, (n.p.: Kypros Press, 2015), loc. 143 of 25738, Kindle.

1. A. B. Simpson, *When the Comforter Came* (Harrisburg, PA: Christian Publications, 1911), 2–3.

2. J. D. Greear, *Jesus Continued* (Grand Rapids, Zondervan, 2014), 25.

3. James David Dickson, "Police continue search for abandon baby's parents," *The Detroit News* online, July 18, 2017, http://www.detroitnews.com/story/news/local/wayne-county/2017/07/18/baby-abandoned-river-rouge-police-seek-tips/103793062/.

4. Cloe Stiller, "How many newborns are discarded in the U.S.? No one knows," *Splinter* online, April 14, 2015, http://splinternews.com/how-many-newborns-are-discarded-in-the-u-s-no-onekno-1793847106.

5. "Facts About Orphans, Refugees and Displaced Children," Orphan Gospel, https://orphangospel.org/facts/facts-about-orphans-refugees-and-displaced-children/.

6. John Piper, "Adoption: The Heart of the Gospel," Desiring God, February 10, 2017, http://www.desiringgod.org/messages/adoption-the-heart-of-the-gospel.

7. Bob Smietana, "Americans love God and the Bible, are fuzzy on the details," LifeWay Newsroom, September 27, 2016, http://blog.lifeway.com/newsroom/2016/09/27/americans-love-god-and-the-bible-are-fuzzy-on-the-details/.

8. Francis Chan, *Forgotten God* (Colorado Springs: David C. Cook, 2009), 70.

9. George S. Hendry, *The Westminster Confession for Today* (Richmond: Knox, 1960), 116–20.

10. Elmer Towns, *The Names of the Holy Spirit* (Ventura, CA: Regal, 1994), 19.

11. J. I. Packer also points out Jesus' repeated use of the masculine pronoun "he" so that readers would be in no doubt that the Spirit is "he," not "it." *Keep in Step with the Spirit* (Old Tappan, NJ: Flemming H. Revell, 1984), 61.

12. Gordon Fee, *Paul, the Spirit, and the People of God* (Peabody, MA: Hendrickson, 1996), 27.

13. A. H. Strong, *Systematic Theology* (Philadelphia: American Baptist Publication Society, 1907), 324.

14. Thomas Goodwin, *The Works of Thomas Goodwin*, volume 8, *The Object and Acts of Justifying Faith* (Edinburgh: James Nichol, 1864), 378–79.

15. Boyd Hunt, *Redeemed! Eschatological Redemption and the Kingdom of God* (Nashville: Broadman and Holman, 1993), 27.

16. Fee, *People of God*, 26.

17. James D. G. Dunn, *Jesus and the Spirit*, (London: SCM Press LTD, 1975), 351.

18. "Omnipresence of God," All About..., https://www.allaboutgod.com/omnipresence-of-god.htm.

19. John Owen, *The Spirit and the Church* (Carlisle, PA: Banner of Truth Trust, 2002), 155.

Practice 5: Worship Like You Are the House of the Lord

Epigraph 1: Colin G. Kruse, *The Gospel According to John: An Introduction and Commentary* (Grand Rapids: William B Eerdmans, 2003), 134–35.

Epigraph 2: Andrew Murray, *The Spirit of Christ* (Minneapolis: Bethany House, 1979), 16–17.

1. D. A. Carson, *The Gospel According to John* (Leicester, England; Grand Rapids: Inter-Varsity Press; W.B. Eerdmans, 1991), 224.

2. George R. Beasley Murray, *The Word Biblical Commentary on John*, vol. 36 (Nashville: Thomas Nelson, 1999), 62.

3. Alan Richardson, *The Gospel According to Saint John: Introduction and Commentary* (London: SCM Press LTD, 1959), 84.

4. David Peterson, *Engaging with God A Biblical Theology of Worship* (Downers Grove, IL: IVP Academic, 1992), 99.

5. D. A. Carson, *Worship by the Book* (Grand Rapids: Zondervan, 2002), 37.

6. William Barclay, *The Gospel of John: Volume 1* (Philadelphia: Westminster Press, 1975), 161.

7. Christopher Ash, *Hearing the Spirit: Knowing the Father through the Son* (London: Christian Focus Publications, 2011), 15.
8. Daniel Henderson, *Fresh Encounters: Experiencing Transformation Through United Worship-Based Prayer* (Colorado Springs: NavPress, 2008).
9. Colin G. Kruse, 133–34.
10. James D. G. Dunn, *Jesus and the Spirit* (London: SCM Press LTD, 1975), 354.
11. John Piper, "Destroy This Temple, and in Three Days I Will Raise It Up," Desiring God, December 21, 2008, http://www.desiringgod.org/messages/destroy-this-temple-and-in-three-days-i-will-raise-it-up.
12. D. A. Carson, *Scandalous: The Cross and Resurrection of Jesus* (Wheaton, IL: Crossway, 2010), 20.
13. Helen Howarth Lemmel, "Turn Your Eyes upon Jesus," 1922, public domain.
14. Peterson, *Engaging with God: A Biblical Theology of Worship*, 201.
15. Harold M. Best, *Unceasing Worship: Biblical Perspectives on Worship and the Arts* (Downers Grove, IL: IVP Books, 2003), 53.

Practice 6: Experience the God Who Already Showed Up

Epigraph 1: A.B. Simpson, *The Holy Spirit or Power From on High, All Volumes* (Brookfield, WI: First Rate Publishers, 2012), 225.
Epigraph 2: D. A. Carson, *Showing the Spirit: A Theological Exposition of 1 Corinthians 12–14* (Grand Rapids: Eerdmans, 1992), 265.
1. My key word here is "teaching" passage. Some point to incidences like Acts 2 where "a sound like a mighty rushing wind" filled the building but the text goes on to distinguish that "they (the gathered believers) were all filled with the Holy Spirit" (Acts 2:3–4). Similarly in Acts 4:31 the place where they gathered was shaken but the believers were "all filled with the Holy Spirit." These manifestations of God's power were notable indeed but in each case, it was the people who were filled with the Spirit.
2. "Power Of God Waits In Church Foyer Until Chorus Of 'Holy Spirit,'" *Babylon Bee*, September 19, 2016, http://babylonbee.com/news/power-god-waits-church-foyer-chorus-holy-spirit/.
3. Robbie Symons, "The Holy Spirit and Freedom!," Harvest Bible Chapel Oakville, March 26, 2017, https://harvestoakville.ca/sermon/the-holy-spirit-and-freedom/.
4. Bob Kauflin, *True Worshipers: Seeking What Matters to God* (Wheaton, IL: Crossway, 2015), 134.
5. See Daniel Henderson, *Transforming Prayer: How Everything Changes When You Seek God's Face* (Minneapolis: Bethany House, 2011), 63.
6. I like to think of this in the way that we might say, "Music filled the atmosphere." This only true because people who were singing and musicians who were playing united their efforts. In other words, song filled the atmosphere because it was coming out of the mouths of individuals who were singing. Notes filled the atmosphere because individuals were playing their instruments. The atmosphere did not produce any music but reflected a communal experience based on the individual efforts. When Christians are filled with the Spirit, expressing the Spirit, ministering in the Spirit, we sense it in the gathering as the assembled people of God.
7. Carl Hoch, *All Things New* (Grand Rapids: Baker, 1995), 232, 236.
8. David Peterson, *Engaging with God: A Biblical Theology of Worship* (Downers Grove, IL: IVP Academic, 1992), 197.
9. Ibid., 198.

10. Norman Grubb, *Continuous Revival: The Secrets of Victorious Living* (Fort Washington, PA: CLC Publications, 1952), 52–53.
11. Ralph P. Martin, in his book *The Family and the Fellowship,* describes four primary church ministry models: 1) The Lecture Room Model, where the focus of ministry is Bible exposition and people come primarily to hear sermons and engage in Bible studies to affirm the correct interpretation and application of Scripture. 2) The Theater Model, where a weekend production is primary and various kinds of performance are featured to emotionally move the crowd. 3) The Large Corporation Model, where the focus is on organization, leadership and programs—usually with an emphasis on growth, more facilities, greater numbers of people and increased financial resources as key indicators of success. 4) The Fellowship Model, where the emphasis is on involvement of all members with a focus on quality sharing with minimal structure and sometimes a distrust of strong leadership. Martin affirms *that* while none of these models is intrinsically wrong, too much emphasis on any one particular model can distort and neglect the important purpose and function of the church. Any one of the models, followed to the exclusion of the others, results in an unbalanced church and a loss of community. An unbalanced church will result in unbalanced Christians. An improper spiritual diet will lead to "spiritual scurvy." (Ralph P. Martin, The Family and the Fellowship (Grand Rapids: Eerdmans, 1979), 112–21.
12. Grubb, *Continuous Revival*, 41.
13. Bill Johnson, *Hosting the Presence: Unveiling Heavens Agenda* (Shippensburg, PA: Destiny Image, 2012), 23.

Practice 7: Seek A "Filling," Not A "Falling"

Epigraph 1: R. A. Torrey, *The R.A. Torrey Collection* (n.p.: Kypros Press 2015), LOC. 136 of 25738, Kindle..
Epigraph 2: John R. Stott, *The Message of Ephesians* (Downers Grove, IL: Intervarsity, 1979), 204.
1. Daniel Iverson, *The UM Hymnal*, No. 393.
2. Meredith Andrews, "Spirit of the Living God," from the album, *Deeper* (Nashville: Word Records, February 19, 2016).
3. "Kari Jobe 'Let Your Glory Fall' Song Story," *Air1*, May 4, 2017, http://www.air1.com/music/news/2017/05/04/kari-jobe-39-let-your-glory-fall-39-song-story.aspx.
4. *The NET Bible First Edition Notes*, Ps 51:11–12, Biblical Studies Press, 2006.
5. For more insight see the excellent book by Leon J. Wood, *The Holy Spirit in the Old Testament* (Grand Rapids: Zondervan, 1976), 53–63.
6. John 16:8–11: "And when he comes, he will convict the world concerning sin and righteousness and judgment: concerning sin, because they do not believe in me; concerning righteousness, because I go to the Father, and you will see me no longer; concerning judgment, because the ruler of this world is judged." The Spirit convicts the lost first of the sin of unbelief, which is the first and root sin of their other unregenerate behavior. He convicts them of righteousness, now that Christ has ascended, showing them their failure to meet God's righteous standard. Third, He convicts them of judgment, as they recognize the judgment of Satan and all sin, and their own condemnation before a holy God unless they repent and believe.
7. The only verse in the New Testament that might be confused for this idea is Titus 3:6 where it speaks of the Holy Spirit "whom he *poured out* on us richly through

Jesus Christ our Savior." Yet, as Gordon Fee states, this "is imagery, pure and simple" (Gordon Fee, *Paul, the Spirit, and the People of God*, 26). The reference is to the internal work the Spirit did in saving us, described in the previous verse as "the washing of regeneration and renewal of the Holy Spirit" (v. 5). Again, there is no command to seek a pouring out (or a falling), only a statement of the fact that we have already experienced this in salvation.

8. In Acts, the "falling" of the Spirit or references to the Spirit "coming upon" people was always in step with the initial understanding of the gospel. This was the indicator of a new work of the Holy Spirit in and among those who would embrace the message of the cross. After the Spirit came and filled the early church on Pentecost, the base of gospel advancement began to spread to other locations, with a vital work of the Spirit, to confirm the advancement of the message of Jesus.

In Acts 8:14–17, the gospel had spread into Samaria through the preaching of Phillip, just as Jesus had declared in Acts 1:8: "But you will receive power when the Holy Spirit has come upon you, and you will be my witnesses in Jerusalem and in all Judea and *Samaria,* and to the end of the earth." To validate the same Pentecostal work of the Holy Spirit which launched the church in Jerusalem, Peter and John went and laid their hands on the new believers for the reception of the Holy Spirit. A true Spirit-empowered, gospel beachhead is now established in Samaria. This is significant because Samaria was the region of half-breed outcasts in the view of the Jewish people.

Much debate exists about whether this is a proof text for the idea that the Holy Spirit is received in some special way after salvation, which is not my focus here. I do like this important clarification offered by Scottish scholar I. H. Marshall. He says that the real point here is "the overcoming of the hostility between the Jews and the Samaritans through their common faith in Jesus, and it is in this sense that the story may be seen as a step towards the greater problem of bringing Jews and Gentiles together. If this is correct, it may provide the clue to the undoubted problem presented by the fact that the Samaritan believers did not receive the Spirit until the apostles laid hands on them. They were thus brought into fellowship with the *whole* church, and not merely with the Hellenist section of it. This explanation is preferable to the view that the Samaritans had not responded fully to the preaching of the gospel" (I. H. Marshall, *Acts: An Introduction and Commentary*, vol. 5 [Downers Grove, IL: InterVarsity Press, 1980], 162).

In Acts 19:1–7 another gospel base is established for the "uttermost parts of the earth" (Acts 1:8 KJV) in the influential pagan city of Ephesus. The work of the good news is taking root among the Gentiles. The apostle Paul is in Ephesus where he encounters some devout followers of John the Baptist who were unaware of the events of Pentecost and, in spite of their devotion to the message of repentance as preached by John, had not even heard of the Holy Spirit. Paul commenced to baptize them into Christ, and the Spirit of God came upon them and filled them in connection with their clarified devotion to Jesus. This divine indicator was important.

9. I have identified one apparent exception in 1 Peter 4:14 where it reads, "If you are insulted for the name of Christ, you are blessed, because the Spirit of glory and of God rests upon you." Here, Peter uses language other than the predominant New Testament teaching on the indwelling of the Holy Spirit. One principle for interpretation is to seek to understand the obscure in light of the obvious. Some commentators explain that Peter is remembering the glory of God that rested on

Jesus and that believers have the same assurance of God's presence through the (indwelling) Holy Spirit. A. T. Robertson gives clarity: "Here the reference is to the Holy Spirit, who is the Spirit of Glory and of God. **Resteth upon you** (επ ημα αναπαυεται). Quotation from Isaiah 11:2. Present middle indicative of αναπαυω, to give rest, refresh (Matthew 11:28). 'He rests upon the Christian as the Shechinah rested upon the tabernacle' (Bigg). Cf. Matthew 1:8; Matthew 3:16" (A. T. Robertson, *Word Pictures in the New Testament* [Nashville, TN: Broadman Press, 1933], https://www.biblestudytools.com/commentaries/robertsons-word-pictures/1-peter/1-peter-4-14.html).

10. Michael Green notes, "What does the New Testament say about the fullness of the Holy Spirit? Surprisingly, it says nothing at all. The Greek word for fullness, *plērōma*, is applied to many things in the New Testament, notably to both Christ and the Church; but never to the Holy Spirit. This is not an important point, because the idea may be present without the word; but it does show how ill-based in Scripture is any attempt to make the 'fulness of the Holy Spirit' into a doctrinal war cry, as if it were a most important and neglected biblical emphasis" (Michael Green, *I Believe in the Holy Spirit* [Grand Rapids: Eerdmans, 1975], 148).

11. Ibid, 149.

12. Ibid.

13. A. B. Simpson, *When the Comforter Came* (Harrisburg, PA: Christian Publications, 1911), 46.

14. Gordon Fee, *God's Empowering Presence: The Holy Spirit in the Letters of Paul* (Peabody, MA: Hendrickson Publishers, 1994), 720.

15. D. Martyn Lloyd-Jones, *Life in the Spirit* (Grand Rapids: Baker, 1973), 46.

16. Ibid., 47.

17. Frank Wallace, "The Holy Spirit In Ephesians: Blessings And Responsibilities," BibleCentre.org, http://biblecentre.org/content.php?mode=7&item=382.

18. Adapted from a statement made by Bryan Chapell about the subject of grace ("Identity and Imitation: Getting First Things First," Crossway, November 14, 2016, https://www.crossway.org/articles/identity-and-imitation-getting-first-things-first/).

19. Klyne Snodgrass, *The NIV Application Commentary* (Grand Rapids: Zondervan, 1996), 301.

20. Jeff Kennedy, *Father, Son and the Other One* (Lake Mary, FL: Passio, 2014), 154.

21. J. I. Packer, *Keep in Step with the Spirit* (Old Tappan, NJ: Flemming H. Revell, 1984), 91.

22. This coincides beautifully with Paul's descriptions of the "manifestation" of the Holy Spirit in 1 Corinthians 12–14, where we Christ followers declare and demonstrate that "Jesus is Lord" (12:3). The same Holy Spirit works by grace in us to uniquely minister unselfishly, in us and through us, for the common good (12:4–12). Accordingly, we cherish the reality of being baptized into one body by the Holy Spirit (12:13). By the power of the Holy Spirit, we honor one another—especially those who seem less important (probably not the ones on the stage). We ultimately regulate all that we do by way of a deep, sacrificial love for one another (13:1–13). Paul goes on to command, "since you are eager for manifestations of the Spirit, strive to excel in building up the church" (14:12). Paul further notes the priority of the proclamation of the Word in convicting and convincing the unbelievers of the power of the presence of God in our midst (14:24–25). He concludes by admonishing that "all things should be done decently and in order" (14:40). Admittedly, this is a very brief summary of some rather sticky chapters, but it's a valid thumbnail of what a Spirit-filled gathering might really look like.

23. Gordon Fee, *God's Empowering Presence: The Holy Spirit in the Letters of Paul* (Peabody, MA: Hendrickson Publishers, 1994), 721.

24. P. T. O'Brien, *The Letter to the Ephesians* (Grand Rapids: W.B. Eerdmans Publishing Co., 1999), 396.

25. Ibid.

26. F. Foulkes, *Ephesians: An Introduction and Commentary*, vol. 10 (Downers Grove, IL: InterVarsity Press, 1989), 158.

Practice 8: Filter the Message in the Music

Epigraph 1: John Piper, "When Worship Lyrics Miss the Mark," Desiring God, August 7, 2017, URL. http://www.desiringgod.org/interviews/when-worship-lyrics-miss-the-mark.

Epigraph 2: Vaughan Roberts, *True Worship* (Bletchley, UK: Authentic Media Group, 2016), 80.

1. Ron Owens with Jan McMurray, *Return to Worship: A God-Centered Approach* (Nashville: Broadman and Holman Publishers, 1999), 139.

2. Serge Denisoff, *Newsweek*, December 30, 1985, p. 54; quoted in Ron Rhodes, "Confusion in Christian Music?," Reasoning from the Scriptures Ministries, http://home.earthlink.net/~ronrhodes/Music.html.

3. "Music and health," Harvard Health Publishing, July 2011, https://www.health.harvard.edu/staying-healthy/music-and-health.

4. Owens, *Return to Worship*, 31.

5. Ed Steele, "'It's a good worship song, but......'" *Worship HeartCries* (blog), September 28, 2015, http://www.edsteeleworship.com/2015/09/its-good-worship-song-but.html, October 27, 2015.

6. D. A. Carson, *Worship by the Book* (Grand Rapids: Zondervan, 2002), 47.

7. Bryan Chapell, *Christ-Centered Worship* (Grand Rapids: Baker Academic, 2009), 130.

8. Daniel Henderson, *PRAYzing! Creative Prayer Experiences from A to Z* (Colorado Springs: NavPress, 2007), 21–61.

9. Ed Steele, *Worship Heartcries* (North Charleston, SC: Ed Steele, 2016), 90.

10. Bill Johnson, *Hosting the Presence* (Shippensburg, PA: Destiny Image Publishers, 2012), 166–67.

11. Bob Kauflin, *True Worshipers: Seeking What Matters to God* (Wheaton, IL: Crossway, 2015), 26–27.

12. Roberts, *Return to Worship*, 75.

13. Vaughn describes the consequences of viewing music as an encounter with God: 1) God's word is marginalized—"Many people do not want to think. They just want to feel God's presence, and they look to music to give them that feeling. But we only encounter God through faith in Jesus, not the music. . . . The spirit of God is the divine author of the Bible and continues to speak through it today." 2) Our assurance is threatened— "Our assurance of God's love does not depend on our feelings. Our assurance instead depends on the finished work of Christ." 3) Musicians are exalted— "They are asked to play a priestly role and bring us into the presence of God by producing an experience. The best Christian musicians . . . will be pointing to Christ and focusing attention on the truth about him." 4) Division is increased— "If we identify an experience with a genuine encounter with God, and only a certain kind of music gives me that experience, then it will be very important to me that that kind of music is played regularly in

my church. . . . If others feel they need different kinds of music, there is bound to be trouble." (69–72)

14. Glenn Packiam, "Are Emotions in Worship Wrong?," Mysteryoffaithblog.com, May 15, 2015, https://mysteryoffaithblog.com/2015/05/15/are-emotions-in-worship-wrong/.

15. Michael Horton, A Better Way: Rediscovering the Drama of Christ-Centered Worship (Grand Rapids: Baker, 2002), 26.

16. See also http://www.strategicrenewal.com/resources/?fwp_types=prayer-guides.

17. "Cambridge Declaration Heritage and Resources," Alliance of Confessing Evangelicals, April 20, 1996, http://www.alliancenet.org/cambridge-declaration. The entirety of the fifth declaration reads:

Soli Deo Gloria: The Erosion of God-Centered Worship
Wherever in the church biblical authority has been lost, Christ has been displaced, the gospel has been distorted, or faith has been perverted, it has always been for one reason: our interests have displaced God's and we are doing his work in our way. The loss of God's centrality in the life of today's church is common and lamentable. It is this loss that allows us to transform worship into entertainment, gospel preaching into marketing, believing into technique, being good into feeling good about ourselves, and faithfulness into being successful. As a result, God, Christ and the Bible have come to mean too little to us and rest too inconsequentially upon us.

God does not exist to satisfy human ambitions, cravings, the appetite for consumption, or our own private spiritual interests. We must focus on God in our worship, rather than the satisfaction of our personal needs. God is sovereign in worship; we are not. Our concern must be for God's kingdom, not our own empires, popularity or success.

Thesis Five: Soli Deo Gloria
We reaffirm that because salvation is of God and has been accomplished by God, it is for God's glory and that we must glorify him always. We must live our entire lives before the face of God, under the authority of God and for his glory alone.

We deny that we can properly glorify God if our worship is confused with entertainment, if we neglect either Law or Gospel in our preaching, or if self-improvement, self-esteem or self-fulfillment are allowed to become alternatives to the gospel.

18. Wiktionary, s.v. "entertainment," last edited February 25, 2018, http://en.wiktionary.org/wiki/entertainment.

19. A. W. Tozer, Alive in the Spirit, 110.

20. Owens, Return to Worship, 25.

21. Many scholars avoid getting too specific on the exact differentiation of "psalms and hymns and spiritual songs." Generally, psalms refer to Old Testament poetry sung with a harp or other songs that had a similar feel. In classical Greek, "hymns" referred to a festive lyric in praise of a god or hero—in this case to Christ. Spiritual songs might be more spontaneous songs from the heart as prompted by the Spirit. Every expression of Christian joy is welcomed, and all should come from the heart—in fact the melody may sometimes be in the heart and not expressed in sound—and go forth addressed to the Lord.

22. One caution: Many of our "songs of testimony" no longer speak of the beauty of Christ and what He has accomplished. Some seem to speak of the impact of

a milquetoast faith and how it has made us feel about ourselves. In the process of writing this book I began to notice how often the personal pronouns of *me*, *my*, and *I* appear in worship songs, not necessarily in reference to our worship of Christ or testimony of the gospel but as a heartwarming statement about how our faith has "improved" our lives. Just a thought.

Practice 9: Enjoy the Gift of Biblical Emotion

Epigraph 1: Jonathan Edwards, *A Treatise Concerning Religious Affections: In Three Parts* (Oak Harbor, WA: Logos Research Systems, Inc., 1996), 5.

Epigraph 2: David Eckman, *The Holy Spirit and Our Emotions;* https://bible.org/seriespage/10-holy-spirit-and-our-emotions.

1. Brian Borgman, "Are Feelings Just the Caboose?," Christianity.com, http://www.christianity.com/bible/are-feelings-just-the-caboose-11602932.html.

2. Some examples include: anger (Matt. 21:12–13; Mark 11:15–17; John 2:14–17), compassion (Matt. 9:36; 14:14; 15:32; 20:34; Mark 1:40-41, 8:2; Luke 7:13), joy and delight (Luke 10:21–24; 15:32; John 15:11; 17:13), grief (Luke 19:41–44; John 11:33, 38), love (John 11:36; 13:1; 15:10; 17:23; 1 John 4:8, 10, 19), deep longing (Luke 22:15).

3. G. Walter Hansen, "The Emotions of Jesus," *Christianity Today*, February 3, 1997, http://www.christianitytoday.com/ct/1997/february3/7t2042.html?order=&start=6.

4. T. D. Lea, *Hebrews, James*, vol. 10 (Nashville, TN: Broadman & Holman Publishers, 1999), 320–21.

5. Herbert Lockyer, *All About the Holy Spirit* (Peabody, MA: Hendrickson Publishers, 1949), 28.

6. Hansen, "The Emotions of Jesus."

7. See Stephen Voorwinde, "Paul's Emotions in 2 Corinthians: Part 1 (Chapters 1-7)," http://www.rtc.edu.au/RTC/media/Documents/Vox%20articles/08-Voorwinde-Paul-s-Emotions-in-2-Corinthians-Part-1-Reviewed.pdf?ext=.pdf. He notes that Paul uses twenty different Greek words to describe his emotions: "No less impressive is the range of emotions expressed. He despairs (1:8), experiences sorrow (2:1, 3; 6:10), is glad (2:2; 12:9, 15), rejoices (2:3; 6:10; 7:4, 7, 9, 13, 16; 13:9), feels anguish of heart (2:4), sheds tears (2:4), loves (2:4; 5:14; 6:6; 11:11; 12:15), is perplexed (4:8), groans (5:2, 4), has regrets (7:8), is afraid (7:5; 11:3; 12:20) and jealous (11:2), mourns (12:21) and burns with distress (11:29). Paul's major emotions in the epistle would therefore seem to be joy/gladness (12x), sorrow (9x) and love (6x). Less common are fear (3x), perplexity/despair (2x) and regret (1x)."

8. Borgman, "Are Feelings Just the Caboose?"

9. Dan Allendar and Tremper Longman, *The Cry of the Soul* (Dallas: Word, 1994), 24–25.

10. D. Martyn Lloyd-Jones, *Spiritual Depression* (Grand Rapids: Eerdmans, 1965), 109.

11. Jon Bloom, "Your Emotions Are a Gauge, Not a Guide," Desiring God, August 3, 2012, https://www.desiringgod.org/articles/your-emotions-are-a-gauge-not-a-guide.

12. Charles Swindoll, *Flying Closer to the Flame* (Dallas: Word Publishing, 1993), 155.

13. Ibid., 155–56.

14. John Piper, *Finally Alive: What Happens When We Are Born Again* (Fearn, Highland: United Kingdom, 2009), 17.
15. Timothy Keller, *Preaching* (New York: Penguin Books, 2015), 157–58.
16. Ibid., 158–59.
17. Ibid., 179.
18. Attributed to John Wesley.
19. Douglas Moo, "Informed Worship," Tabletalk, October 2012.
20. David Eckman, *The Holy Spirit and Our Emotions*, https://bible.org/seriespage/10-holy-spirit-and-our-emotions.
21. Glenn Packiam, "Are Emotions in Worship Wrong?," *Church Leaders*, July 5, 2017, https://churchleaders.com/worship/worship-articles/306192-emotions-worship-wrong-glenn-packiam.html.
22. Arturo Azurdia, *Spirit Empowered Preaching* (Geanies House, United Kingdom: Christian Focus, 2015), 48.
23. J. I. Packer, *Keep in Step with the Spirit* (Old Tappan, NJ: Fleming H. Revell, 1984), 67.
24. Vaughan Roberts, *True Worship* (Bletchley, UK: Authentic Media Group, 2016), 74.
25. Ed Steele, "What About Emotions and Worship?," *Worship HeartCries* (blog), July 19, 2017, http://www.edsteeleworship.com/2017/07/what-about-emotions-and-worship.html.
26. Ed Steele, "Worship and Entertainment," *Worship HeartCries* (blog), March 1, 2010, http://www.edsteeleworship.com/2010/03/worship-and-entertainment-church-that.html.
27. John Piper, "God Seeks People to Worship Him in Spirit and Truth," Desiring God, April 8, 1984, http://www.desiringgod.org/messages/god-seeks-people-to-worship-him-in-spirit-and-truth.

Practice 10: Maximize the Holy Spirit's Life Plan

Epigraph 1: Adoniram Judson Gordon, as quoted in *They Found the Secret* (Grand Rapids: Zondervan, 1977), 64.
Epigraph 2: Herbert Lockyer *All About the Holy Spirit* (Peabody, MA: Hendrickson Publishers, 1995), 28.
1. J. I. Packer, *Keep in Step with the Spirit* (Old Tappan, NJ: Flemming H. Revell, 1984), 19.
2. Just in case you are not convinced of the supremacy of the new covenant, I highly recommend you continue your own Spirit-guided study until you are clear and compelled to understand a truly gospel view of the Holy Spirit. Again, I would compel you to read and embrace Paul's teaching in 2 Corinthians 3:1–4:6. Digest the truths of Hebrews 7–13 (especially Hebrews 8). A few helpful books I would recommend are: *The Spirit of Christ* by Andrew Murray; *The Two Covenants* by Andrew Murray; *All Things New* by Carl B. Hoch Jr.; *The Presence of God* by J. Ryan Lister; *Covenant, Community and the Spirit* by Robert Sherman; and, if you are able to find it, a very technical book: *Moses' Veil and The Glory of the New Covenant* by Carol Kern Stockhausen. The more you grasp this, the greater your appreciation will be for the sufficiency of the work of Christ and the power of the indwelling Holy Spirit. You will begin to understand your Christian life through a new covenant lens.
3. Andrew Murray, *The Two Covenants* (San Bernardino, CA: Andrew Murray, 2017), 54.

4. Jim Hughes, "Each New Day by Corrie ten Boom," http://each-new-day-corrie-ten-boom.blogspot.com/2012/05/may-15.html.
5. Michael Horton, *Rediscovering the Holy Spirit* (Grand Rapids: Zondervan, 2017), 26.
6. The New Testament contains scores of descriptions of our new identity in Christ. All of these are the result of our new life in Christ and the indwelling power of the Holy Spirit. See http://www.giveittogodbbq.com/uploads/3/4/9/7/34979933/90_statements.pdf.
7. "Martin Luther," ReligionFacts, www.religionfacts.com/martin-luther.
8. Frank Logsdon, *The Lord of the Harvest: The Manifestation and Ministration of the Holy Spirit* (Grand Rapids: Zondervan, 1954), 7.

Conclusion: Pursuing the Hope of a New Covenant Revival

Epigraph 1: As quoted by Stephen Olford, *Heart Cry for Revival* (Memphis, TN: Christian Focus, 2015), 47.
Epigraph 2: Stephen Olford, *Heart Cry for Revival* (Memphis, TN: Christian Focus, 2015), 94.
1. One common proof text is from Peter's sermon in Acts 3:19–20, where he exclaimed to the Jewish audience on the day of Pentecost, "Repent therefore, and turn back, that your sins may be blotted out, that times of refreshing may come from the presence of the Lord, and that he may send the Christ appointed for you, Jesus." Various interpretations have been given for "times of refreshing may come from the presence of the Lord." Clearly, in context, this was a call to salvation to the lost Jews, not a teaching on revival for the church. Some view this as a reference to the future millennium. At best, it could be viewed as a description of the "cooling off that comes from blowing, like the refreshment of a cool breeze" (the literal meaning) that comes with salvation, along with the forgiveness and cleansing that Peter references in this evangelistic sermon. We might say that "the presence of the Lord" referenced here is always a source of "refreshing." If so, must be the reality of the indwelling Holy Spirit, according the new covenant.
2. *Merriam-Webster*, s.v. "revive," last updated April 21, 2018, https://www.merriam-webster.com/dictionary/revive.
3. Bill Hull, *Revival That Reforms* (Grand Rapids: Fleming H. Revell, 1998), 17, 19.
4. Ibid., 19.
5. Iain H. Murray, *Revival and Revivalism* (Carlisle, PA: Banner of Truth, 1994), 376.
6. Iain H. Murray, *Pentecost – Today?: The Biblical Basis for Understanding Revival* (Carlisle, PA: Banner of Truth, 1998), 23–24.
7. Richard Owen Roberts, *Revival* (Wheaton, IL: Richard Owen Roberts Publishers, 1997), 16.
8. Norman Grubb, *Continuous Revival: The Secret of Victorious Living* (Fort Washington, PA: CLC Publications, 1952), 61.
9 Ibid., 10.
10. Ibid., 18–21.
11. D. Martyn Lloyd-Jones, *Spiritual Depression* (Grand Rapids: Eerdmans, 1965), 108.
12. Jim Cymbala, "How to Light the Fire," *CT Pastors*, May 19, 2004, http://www.christianitytoday.com/pastors/books/preachingworship/lclead01-22.html.
13. Olford, *Heart Cry for Revival*, 69.
14. Norman Grubb, *Continuous Revival: The Secret of Victorious Living* (Fort Washington, PA: CLC Publications, 1952), 9.

15. Olford, *Heart Cry for Revival*, 80.

16. Robert E. Coleman, cited in Walter C. Kaiser Jr., *Revive Us Again* (Nashville: Broadman and Holman, 1999), ix.

17. Andrew Murray, *The Spirit of Christ* (Minneapolis: Bethany House, 1979), 8–9.

Appendix 1: Accurately Applying the Actions of Acts

1. Gordon D. Fee and Douglas Stuart, *How to Read the Bible for All It's Worth* (Grand Rapids: Zondervan, 2009), 124.

2. J. B. Polhill, *Acts*, vol. 26 (Nashville: Broadman & Holman Publishers, 1992), 98.

Appendix 2: A New Covenant Worship Vocabulary

1. Howard Marshall, in the preface to David Peterson, *Engaging with God* (Downers Grove, IL: IVP Academic, 1992), 9.

ACKNOWLEDGMENTS

Individually, we are all but a note. In harmony with others we become part of a beautiful symphony. While I played my note in the writing of this book, many others have helped make this project, and the other dimensions of our ministry, a Christ-honoring orchestration.

Rosemary, my partner in marriage for over thirty-five years, once again demonstrated amazing patience and grace. As the time-consuming task of writing a book was added to our already-busy lives, she has carried an extra load without complaint.

The staff of Strategic Renewal grew our multifaceted ministry efforts during the countless hours of my obsession with this project. Thank you Jordan, Shannon, Carley, Robert, and Todd for your support.

The board of Strategic Renewal continued to show such gracious encouragement and prayer support. Thank you Tony, Scott, Josh, Ann, Jim, Joel, Ed, Brett, Tim W., Tim, and Michelle for your partnership.

Larry Page provided a beautiful venue that inspired my writing at a crucial stage in this project. Pastor Cary Hughes burned the midnight oil in some very helpful proofreading and editing during the final hours. Pastor Sandy Robertson and Jordan Henderson provided a wide array of books that were profoundly helpful.

Jim Cymbala's friendship has given me a fresh interest in the work of the Holy Spirit through the model of his life and ministry. For this, I am exceedingly grateful.

One author, in particular, has been a profound help in shaping my thoughts. Andrew Murray and his book, *The Spirit of Christ*, kick-started my passion for this project. Others, including Norman Grubb, Carl Hoch, Larry Pettegrew, and Gordon Fee, provided unique inspiration.

Our ministry prayer partners are the heroes behind the scenes, serving like Aaron and Hur, lifting up my hands in faithful intercession. Only eternity will reveal the profound influence of these praying friends.

The team at Moody Publishers has been extraordinary in so many ways. Duane Sherman's thoughtful guidance and continued encouragement blessed me immeasurably. Connor Sterchi's editing efforts brought clarity and balance to the content. Many others at Moody have played a vital role in the completion of this project.

My deepest gratitude, love, and worship for my Lord Jesus Christ remains paramount. His fully sufficient work at Calvary and glorious resurrection-life has supplied the gift beyond description. The person and presence of the Holy Spirit indwelling me, continues to transform me, from the inside out. Praise His name!

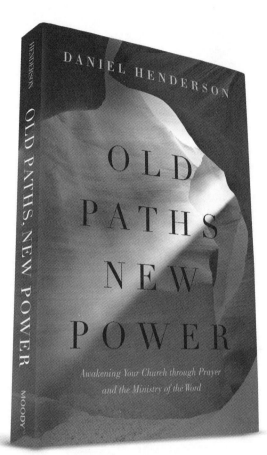

ENCOUNTER GOD. WORSHIP MORE.

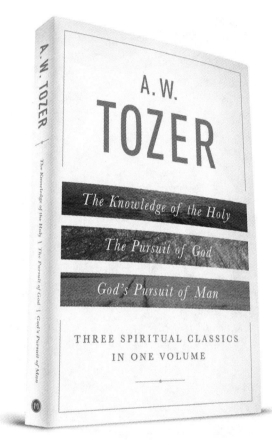

MOODY
Publishers®

*From the Word **to** Life*®

Considered to be Tozer's greatest works, *The Knowledge of the Holy*, *The Pursuit of God*, and *God's Pursuit of Man* are now available in a single volume. In *Three Spiritual Classics*, you will discover a God of breathtaking majesty and world-changing love, and you will find yourself worshipping through every page.

978-0-8024-1861-6

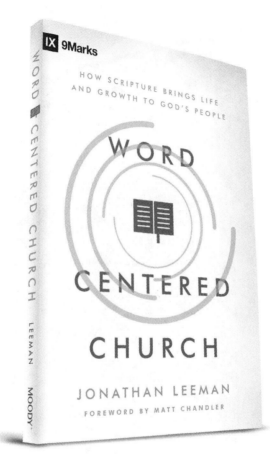

WHEN CHURCH AND CULTURE LOOK THE SAME...

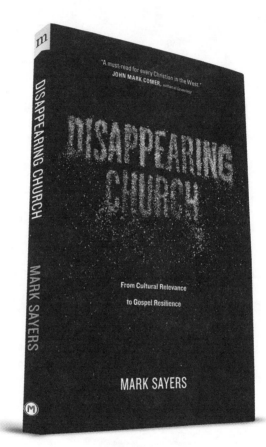

STRATEGIC RENEWAL

Experience real transformation through Strategic Renewal's coaching process.

With author Daniel Henderson as your coach, you will find true breakthrough in your spiritual life and gain tools to build a life and ministry that seeks God and experiences His power.

Our coaching is more than just imparting information. It is a dynamic, interactive process that helps unlock your full potential, taking you from where you are to where God wants you to be.

COACHING OPTIONS

30 DAYS TO PERSONAL RENEWAL: Discover new and biblical spiritual disciplines that will renovate the framework of your life and restore fresh engagement with God.

90 DAYS TO PASTORAL EMPOWERMENT: Gain the leadership tools and principles needed to see God develop a vibrant, healthy, Spirit-empowered church.

180 DAYS TO CHURCH TRANSFORMATION: Experience supernatural impact as you equip your leadership, staff, and entire congregation to cultivate a community that seeks God.

For more information visit **strategicrenewal.com/coaching**

Strategic Renewal exists to serve the local church and its leaders by catalyzing personal transformation and leadership health through events, resources, and a variety of interactive coaching experiences.